INCLUSIVE GROWTH IN INDIA

Contents

Preface

This book "Inclusive Ggrowth in India" is the outcome of scholarly deliberations made on the eve of 11th annual conference of Economic Association of Bihar and Jharkhand (EABJ) held in April, 2008 at the College of Commerce, Patna. India has made progress to the large extent under the different Five Year Plans. But the outcome of development could not reach the last person of the society. There are vast inequalities and disparities at inter-personal, inter-regional, rural-urban and gender levels. It is curse in the way of planned development of India. The approach paper of 11th Five Year Plan is named as "Towards Faster and More Inclusive Growth." The word 'Inclusive Growth' was discussed in the Asian Development Bank (ADB) Conference (Oct., 2007) also in its "Forum on Inclusive Growth and Poverty Reduction." In the "India Development Report, 2006" published by the World Bank it is mentioned the development process is not only the index of the sum total of all economic activities, but it is the evaluation of inclusiveness of economic development. Under the inclusive development not only the distribution of economic benefits is considered, but social security, empowerment and the feeling of full participation are attained. The both main objectives of economic growth:

(1) Reform in the distribution of main services, and
(2) More inclusive growth are depended on empowerment and creation of opportunities for each individual.

Inclusive growth directs towards such economic

development in which benefits of high rate of gross domestic development-oriented national income may reach the weakest classes of the society equally. Geographically all regions/ sectors of nation may travel together in the race of development. The economic inequalities should be the least and the basic amenities like pure drinking water, nutritious food, health, and education, unpolluted environment may reach to all equally. There is need of 'inclusive growth strategy.' Without it we cannot be able to invest properly for the social infrastructure specially on health and primary education for all under the public sector. Inclusive growth as dealt with in our Eleventh Plan means not excluding any section of the society. The aim is to have a fast and inclusive growth for the entire economy. The benefits of development should reach to all.

Inclusiveness has four attributes—

(a) Opportunity,
(b) Capability,
(c) Access, and
(d) Security.

Inclusive Growth is a process in which, measured by a sustained expansion in GDP Contributes to an enlargement of the scale and scope of all four dimensions. Presently Indian economy is full of faith and optimism. The ruins of old economy have already disappeared. This is essential to have attention on two issues for having economy on the path of high rate growth on sustainable basis.

(a) To make high growth rate sustainable by controlling inflation at normal level.
(b) The nature of high growth rate may certainly be inclusive so that its benefits may reach the all classes/sections of society and all regions/sectors of the country equally.

The approach paper of our recent plan is based on two economic theories:

(a) The high rate of growth is essential not for only raising the standard of living, but also for creating more opportunities of employment.
(b) For inclusive growth it is not only essential to increase financial allotments for social sectors only, it is also essential to protect the life of the people.

No one may doubt in those facts that either our share index may jump to over 21,000 or our foreign currency reserve fund may have more than 307 Arab dollar ($) or our GDP may increase by the rate of 9.6 percent annually, which may record our economy in the category of fastly growing economies, but with this high rate of growth when our country is facing large rate of prevailing unemployment, acute poverty, malnutrition, disease, illiteracy, etc. that show that our current development is not inclusive in any way at all. Our country is divided into two parts—India and Bharat. India represents the urban as well as industrial sector and Bharaṭ represents rural as well as agricultural sector. Mahatma Gandhi said that Bharat resides in its more than 5.5 lakh villages (not in more than 20,000 towns only). Indian agriculture not only creates employment opportunities for more than two-third (2/3) population, but it supplies the raw materials for our industries also.

For tertiary sector the rural and agricultural sector provides a large market. In this position if the growth rate of agricultural sector remains around 2.4 percent, it is indicator of this fact that the real income of the 70-75 crore population does not increase and those people are unable to get the benefits of high rate of growth. There is wide gap between the agriculture and industries as well as service sectors. There had become remarkable development-based divide-line between the eastern parts (all states of north-east, W. Bengal, Bihar, Jharkhand and Orissa) and western parts (Punjab, Haryana, Gujarat, Maharashtra) of India. In the race of development Orissa, Bihar, Jharkhand, Assam, Manipur, Mizoram, Tripura, Arunanchal Pradesh, Meghalaya, Madhya Pradesh, Eastern U.P., a large part of Andhra Pradesh are lagging behind (are very backward). The standard of living of the persons living in those states is very low and they are not seen beneficiaries and participants in the high growth rate generated benefits. If along with the targeted 9-10 per cent growth rate GDP targeted, 4.0 per cent growth rate of agriculture sector is attained also, the gap between agriculture and non-agriculture income will be widened. If this gap is to be reduced, the increase of more than 5 per cent in non-agriculture employments is must because more than two-third (2/3) population of the country is depended on agriculture, the slow rate of growth in agriculture will not make limit the area of domestic market, but in future the industries will have to face many obstacles in the development of wage-goods. So the development of agriculture must be the first priority of economy marching towards high growth.

We think, this book will be beneficial for those policy-makers, planners, statisticians, politicians, economists and research scholars in the fields of planning and development as well as for those who are worse-off in the race of development as they may search their path of development and may have their real participation in development.

ANIL KUMAR THAKUR
RAM UDDESHYA SINGH

List of Contributors

Abhas Saurabh, Research Associate, Research Institute for Rural Development, Hajipur, Vaishali, Bihar.

Bharat Bushan, Lecturer in the Department of Economics, T.S. College, Hisua (Nawada).

Bharti Kumari, Research Associate, Research Institute for Rural Development, Hajipur, Vaishali, Bihar.

Birendra Kumar Jha, Reader and Head, Deptt. of Economics, D.B.K.N. College, Narhan, Samastipur, Bihar.

D.M. Diwakar, Professor of Economics at Giri Institute of Development Studies, Lucknow, Uttar Pradesh.

Dayanidhi Prasad Roy, Proctor, L.N.M.U., Dharbhanga.

G.M. Bhat, Prof. and Head, Post Graduate Department of Economics, University of Kashmir, Srinagar-190006.

Jayanti Ningombam, D.M. College of Commerce, Government of Manipur, Imphal.

Kabita Kumari, MA in Economics, Magadh University, Bodh Gaya.

Mahesh Chandra Prasad, Senior Lecturer, Department of Applied Economics and Commerce, Patna University, Patna.

Md. Tarique, Lecturer, University Deptt. of Economics B.R.Ambedkar Bihar University, Muzaffarpur.

Padmini Prasad, Lecturer, P.G. Dept. of Commerce, College of Commerce, Patna, Bihar.

R.U. Singh, Lecturer, P.G. Dept. of Commerce, College of Commerce, Patna, Bihar.

Sangeeta, Research Scholar, Dept. of Political Science, Magadh University, Bodh Gaya, Bihar.

Sanjay Kumar, Research Scholar, Dept. of Political Science, Magadh University, Bodh Gaya, Bihar.

Shabir Ahmad Padder, Research Fellow, Post Graduate Department of Economics, University of Kashmir, Srinagar-190006.

Shekhar, H.O.D. in Psychology, S.S. College Mehus (Shekhpura).

Tikendrajit Poonam, D.M. College of Commerce, Government of Manipur, Imphal.

Zafar Ahmad Sultan, Lecturer, P.G. Dept. of Economics, L.S. College, Muzaffarpur, B.R.A. Bihar University, Muzaffarpur, Bihar.

Introduction

This book entitled 'Inclusive Growth in India' is based on one of the four topics for discussion in the 11th annual conference of ' Economic Association of Bihar and Jharkhand' (EABJ) held in April 2008 in the College of Commerce, Patna. Our Planning Commission introduced different plans with different adjectives such as 'Growth with Poverty Reduction', Growth with Social Justice', 'Growth with Equity' and so on. The approach paper of 11th Five Year Plan is named as 'Towards Faster and More Inclusive Growth'. The discussion took place among the renowned economists and scholars. The book includes thirteen papers. There are altogether eighteen writers. Nine papers are written by Single author, three by two each and one by three authors. The book focuses on the view that all corners of the nation should have share in the development. **Dr. Montek Singh Ahluwalia**, the great economist and the Deputy Chairman of Planning Commission of India stressed on the view that such strategy which ignores the economic growth is not sustainable. But he ignores the human face of development. We should guarantee that the benefits of development should be spread over all directions.

The first author **Ram Naresh Thakur** in his paper 'Unequal Development—A Challenge for Inclusive Growth' stresses on the inequality spread over different part of India as well as in rural and urban sectors. He expresses his view that the high rate of growth is essential not for only raising the standard of some people, but also for creating more opportunities of employment and income generation. For fulfilling these objectives it is essential to bring change in the policies, to activate the bureaucracy more and more and to execute insurance polices for the un-organized sector, which had rapid growth character. The poverty is increasing tremendously in rural areas; the poverty rate is not reducing rapidly. A lot of population is suffering from lack of minimum basic needs, viz. housing problem, hunger, mal-nutrition, diseases, illiteracy, health, education and drinking water, etc. Those agonies are named as 'agony of equality'. **Birendra Kumar Jha** has the opinion that it is not easy to say how much of poverty alleviation has taken place due to the programmes of poverty alleviation and how much due to economic growth itself. He expresses his view that the growth process by itself needs not result in the eradication of poverty since the benefits of the growth may go to those sections of the society who are already better-off. He has analysed the poverty of Bihar and suggested ways to eliminate it. **D.M. Diwakar** focuses on the retarding growth prospects of agriculture in absence of reforms. He expresses his view that realisation of the implementation of land reforms in Bihar unfolds many dimensions, which were responsible for the failures. He further says that India is the only country where the judiciary has played a crucial role in frustrating and stultifying land reforms. Disparities with increasing social tensions and corresponding state repressions are going to be the order of the future of Bihar, where poor peasants will have less democratic space to raise their voice. **G.M. Bhat** and **Shabir Ahmad Padder** make analysis of inclusive growth in the globalised India. They have also discussed the challenges and options. They say that Indian economy is on cross-roads. There are inter-personal and inter-regional disparities. There are gaps between different social groups in India, more glaring in case of SCs, STs and minorities. They suggested measures to meet this gap. According to **Abhas Saurabh** and **Bharti Kumari** 'making growth and development inclusive has become a challenge for planners and policy-makers in India. He says that no doubt, development has taken place, but the process has been too slow. Despite the overall objectives of inclusive growth, the discussion on employment has been the core of the Eleventh Plan. **Mahesh Chandra Prasad** in his article 'the process of economic growth in India' explains that the provision of food security, employment and education for all is likely to greater problem than ever before. He suggests that the investment in agriculture needs be stepped up especially in the lagging regions. The backward and forward linkages in agriculture in poorer regions need to be emphasized more. **Md. Tarique** has emphasized the role of agriculture in attaining inclusive growth in India. He opined that the key components of the 'inclusive growth' strategy must include sharp increase in investment in rural areas, rural infrastructure and agriculture; spurt in credit for farmers; increase in rural employment through a unique social safety net; and sharp increase in public spending on education and health care. The vision for inclusive growth lies in empowering the poor. **Padmini Prasad** has made analysis of strategy for accelerated and inclusive growth for Indian economy with special focus on agriculture. He observes that pushing up radical reforms always requires a strong political will as it challenges the interests of privileged groups. In the wake of global showdown, India must look inwards and lead the world. **R.U. Singh** and **Sangeeta** highlighted the inclusive growth and economic development along with challenges and prospect. They explain inclusive growth as dealt with our 11th Plan means not excluding any section of the society. The aim is to have a fast and inclusive growth of the entire economy. The benefits of development should reach all. **Sanjay Kumar** has dealt with the economic growth in India and pattern of distribution. According to him this uneven growth has been creating a wide ditch between not only poor and richer sectors of people but also among states and inside the states. It is surprising that World Bank has expressed a country report that economic growth and economic disparity are *sine qua non* for development. If this logic is accepted, then the objective of employment generation and altering the condition of poor people have no relevance. **Tikendrajit Paonam** and **Jayanti Ningombam** have dwelt upon the indudustrial development path of less developed regions in the globalised economy in special reference to north eastern region of India. They observe that the world economy has been undergoing unprecedented changes leading to emergence of market driven society. This has necessitated structural adjustment internationally as demanded by the forces influencing global business environment. They have analysed that the north eastern region (NER) of India consisting of eight states, viz. Assam, Arunachal Pradesh, Manipur, Meghalaya, Mizoram, Tripura and Sikkim has got its definite identity due to its peculiar physical, economic and socio-cultural characteristics. **Zafar Ahmad Sultan** has synthesized the poverty, inequality and inclusive growth in India. He explains that the pace of poverty reduction depends not only on the rate of economic growth but also how the benefits of this growth are shared. According to him, Indian development experience has been characterized by rising income and expenditure inequalities and stubbornly high levels of non-income inequalities. Various dimensions of economic and social disparity—regional, rural-urban, social class, inter-personal and gender have aggravated in the recent period. He further suggests if the things go well in the desired direction as is conceived in the plan, may to some extent, lessen some of these disturbing outcomes of the reform period. **Bharat Bhushan, Shekher** and **Kabita Kumari** explain economic development, problems and prospects of weaker section of society in Bihar. According to them, economic development implies the process of securing level of productivity in all sectors of economy and this in turn, is a function of the level of technology, the Bihar economy is required to forge the physical apparatus in the form of machines, equipments, tools and instruments of production on the one hand and on the other, to train the labour force of the state of Bihar and India to make use of physical apparatus thus created. They are optimistic for the poorer, marginalised and weaker section of the society, dalit and minority of Bihar because the present C.M., **Mr. Nitish Kumar** is very prompt to abolish the poverty from Bihar and make Bihar a developed state of India as he has political will to make inclusive growth. **Dayanidhi Prasad Roy** in his article discusses the inclusive inequality and the Indian farmer.

This book will be very useful for understanding the concept of inclusive growth for the scholars, readers, planners and policy-makers. As India is facing vast inequalities and disparities socially and economically, the guidelines inherent in this book will show them path for fulfilling those objectives so that to establish a society full of equity, social justice and to eliminate the unequal growth. If the planners and policy-makers bring changes in policies, to activate the bureaucracy more and more and to execute the plans honestly with a view to fulfill these objectives, there will be no late to make the growth inclusive.

ANIL KUMAR THAKUR
RAM UDDESHYA SINGH

Unequal Development—A Challenge for Inclusive Growth

RAM NARESH THAKUR

The approach paper of 11th Five Year Plan is named as "Towards Faster And More Inclusive Growth". The word "Inclusive Growth" was discussed in the Asian Development Bank (ADB) Conference (Oct. 2007) also in its "Forum on Inclusive Growth and Poverty Reduction". The word 'Inclusive Growth' means such development in which resource may be distributed among all classes of society equally along with its advantages. This simply means such development in which each section of the society has its share. According to it there should be sustainable development having diversified approach. The development should be for all. The approach paper of our recent plan is based on two economic theories:

(i) The high rate of growth is essential not for only raising the standard of living, but also for creating more opportunities of employment.

(ii) For inclusive growth it is not only essential to increase financial allotments for social sectors only, it is also essential to protect the life of people.

For fulfilling these objectives it is essential to bring changes in policies, to activate the bureaucracy more and more and to execute insurance policies for the unorganised sector which has rapid growth character. The poverty is increasing tremendously in rural areas, the poverty rate is not reducing rapidly, a lot of population is suffering from lack of minimum basic needs viz. housing problem, health, education, drinking water, etc. Lacs of children are victimised of mal-nutrition. Those agonies are named as 'agony of equality'

Our Country is divided into two parts—India and Bharat. Bharat, i.e. the nation of the rural people and India represents urban people. The major part of the poor consists of rural poor. The government data shows that there became only 8 percent decrease in the number of persons of below poverty line between 1993-94 to 2004-05. That means the poverty reduces in the very slow rate, i.e. 0.75 per annum. In 1993-94 the ratio of the persons of below poverty line in the total population was 36 percent, which reduced up to 28 percent in 2004-05. It is wonder that the 'poverty line' is not the line of 'poverty' but it is the 'line of hunger', 'The line of extreme poverty. The U.N.O. recognises $ 2 (Rs. 90) per capita per day expenditure as 'poverty line' and 32 percent persons come under this line in India. Unemployment has also been increasing rapidly. In 1993-94 the 'rate of rural unemployment for men' was 5.6 percent, which increased up to 9 percent in 2004. In the same span of period the 'rate of rural unemployment for women' was also 5.6 percent, which increased up to 9.3 percent. In the same way this rate of unemployment of urban male became 8.1 percent increasing from 6.7 percent between 1993-94 to 2004. This rate became 11.7 percent increased from 10.5 percent for the urban female. This rate is the incident of that very period when the market value of the total shares listed in the share market became Rs.16,98,428 crore (in 2004-05) increased from Rs. 1,88,146 crore (in 1993-94).

In other hand, during the financial year 2005-06, there became tremendous increase in the number of such persons having more than $ 10 lac (More than > Rs. 5 crore) financial assets, e.g. shares, bonds, saving bonds, etc. This speed is the

TABLE 1

Rural-Urban Unemployment Rate

	Rural Unemployment Rate in (%)		*Urban Unemployment Rate in (%)*	
	Male	*Female*	*Male*	*Female*
1993-94	5.6	5.6	6.7	10.7
2003-04	9	9.3	8.1	11.7

TABLE 2

Market value of Total Shares Listed in the Share Market

(In Rs. Crore)

1993-94	1,88,146
2003-04	16,98,428

second biggest in the world. Such persons are 83,000 in number. This number was 61,000 in 2003 and 71,000 in 2004. These 83,000 persons are the owners (lords, masters) of $290 Arab, i.e. at least the financial assests of Rs. 14,00,000 crore. These 83,000 big persons have grip over the 40 percent of gross domestic product (GDP) of India on the market value. These 83,000 big persons covers only 0.01 percent of total adult population of India.

The leaders of the nations are in hurry to go forward at any cost, but they are not ready to leave the neo-liberal policies. This is only the 'so-called reform' which is in the root of such tremendous unemployment due to which the

TABLE 3

Rapid Increase of Billionaires

2003	61000
2004	71000
2005	83000

public health facilities has decreased to the negligible point. Rural life is infested with epedemics, illness and ill health. Malnutrition has become the main problem. One, out of two children, dies due to malnutrition. This is the same 'reform' due to which more than a lac persons were compelled to do sucide in Andhra Pradesh, Karnataka, Maharashtra, Punjab and other states during previous fifteen years of globalisation era. It is the same 'reform' due to which thousands of farmers and peasants are over-thrown from the ownership of their land. It is the same 'reform' due to which the 'Special Economic Zones (SE2)' are being established which will throw lacs of workers in the ditch of unemployment.

In the 11th Five Year Plan government will spend heavy amount of money on 'poverty eradication'. The number of big cars and other vehicles will be increased on the roads. There will be increase in the magnificent buildings of thousands of people. There will be good management for the luxuries of future generations of some persons. Some pieces of loaves will reach to the poors also. But will there be any qualitative change really in the lots of those poors ? The 'Eradicate poverty' or 'Garibi Hatao' slogans or stunts of the governments could not remove the poverty and the soil-rooted truth of the 'rural india' or the 'real India.' Any government could not take any chronic or stable step to save the existence of the 'rural India'. It could not change the fate of those people facing always with horrible poverty, unemployment, hunger, malnutrition and illness, etc. The share market of the country is creating new records daily, the foreign exchange stocks are increasing day by day, growth rate is focussing of development, the condition of industries is better than before, the profits of some companies increased upto 50 percent. The Tata steel is taking over the four times big British-Dutch company 'chorus'. The prosperousness of the industrial sector or urban India is visible on the screen. But the 'face of the rural India' is not such. What ever the government is doing is not for 'the welfare of rural India, not for 'the development of rural India,' not to attract 'the rural people of India', but to attract 'the innocent poor voters related with villages'. This is the real agony. In the remote villages poors are being poorer on the cost of some rich

people. The gap of disparity is widening day by day. Our Prime Minister says, "there will not be a poor person in coming 20 years." But the reality is such that the Planning Commission has prepared the 11th Plan (2007-12) in such a way that our agriculture will be prosperous in future five years if one crore farmers will adopt other professions leaving agriculture. That means 20 lakh farmers should tell good-bye to agriculture each year. What will be the employment/profession of those 20 lakh farmers leaving agriculture every year? The Planning Commission has no answer to this question. Those one crore farmers will add the number of large volume of unemployeds waiting from before. The Planning Commission of India can not have the different views except the eminent economists, the planners of the policies of globalisation. The majority of the rural people are facing with the regular increasing problems. They are struggling for the 'Crisis of existence' only. The inequality of 'urban growth rate' and 'rural growth rate' of 8 and 2 percent respectively tells the real story of rural India. The Planning Commission of India is of opinion that the 'slow growth rate' of agriculture cannot be increased in comparison of that of industries. Hence the suicide made by the farmers is impossible to be prevented. It is only why the Planning Commission suggests farmers to leave the profession of agriculture.

COST AND PRICE DISPARITY OF AGRICULTURAL AND INDUSTRIAL GOODS

What will be fate of those rural people or farmers who will march to urban areas in search of jobs ? What will be of their basic amenities of life? The price of every commodity (except agricultural) has increased 200 to 300 times in respect of 1978. There is no sequence of balance in 'Cost determination' and 'price fixation,' nor the government has any control/interference/command on it. Really it is only the central point of 'the conspiracy to break the rural economy'. It is impossible to be checked by the governments governed by the industrialists/entrepreneurs and capitalists. So a farmer, a common rural Indian cannot afford to buy

TABLE 4

Incidence of Poverty Level—Social and Occupational Group (Rural)

Category	*Incidence (%)*			
	Very Poor		*Poor*	
	1993-94	*1994-00*	*1993-94*	*1994-00*
Caste				
ST	22.1	17.0	50.2	44.2
SC	22.7	11.5	48.3	23.3
OBC	NA	7.0	NA	25.5
Occupation				
Agricultural Labour	26.2	14.1	54.4	39.7
Non-agricultural Labour	15.2	8.7	42.2	27.2

Source: Computed using NSS 50th Round Data on Household Consumer Expenditure.

industrial goods. He lacks the purchasing power (entitlement) to purchase the industrial produces. In other hand, he has to sell agricultural goods/produce on cheap prices. The difference of 'initial cost' and 'Selling cost' of agricultural goods is rarely 1.5 to 2 times, whereas this goes upto 10 times in the case of industrial goods (Produces). If the cost of steel is Rs. 30 per Kg., but its utensils of reputed companies are sold Rs. 300 per Kg. But in villages if the cost of the raw material of any matter (e.g. soil pot) is Rs. 100, the pot will be sold in Rs. 150 per Kg. maximum. Thus the cottage/household industries are being smashed by the big industries.

The lives of the crores of people of rural India is worsening for maintaining the 'growth rate' of few crores of people of urban India. The development models of western/developed (south) countries will not be suited for the proper development of rural India. We should think property for the 'existence of rural India'.

The occupational composition of the rural poor varied across the states. In general, in the developed states poverty was highly concentrated among agricultural labour households and, in contrast, in the backward states poverty extended to other occupational groups, including the self-employed in agriculture. For instance, in Punjab, Haryana, Maharashtra, and Andhra Pradesh agricultural labour households constituted more than 60 percent of the rural poor in 1999-2000, but they constituted less than 16 percent in Rajasthan and 28 percent in Assam.

Among the social groups, SCs, STs, and backward castes accounted for 81 percent of the rural poor in 1999-2000 whereas they were considerably less among the rural population. The poor among the SCs in rural areas were concentrated in Uttar Pradesh, Bihar and West Bengal. They comprised 58 percent of the poor among SCs. In urban areas, Madhya Pradesh and Uttar Pradesh accounted for 41 percent of the poor among the SCs. The incidence of poverty among SCs was high in Bihar, Madhya Pradesh, and Uttar Pradesh in both rural and urban areas. In terms of income poverty and other indicators of human development also such as education, health, etc., the STs are at the bottom. The increasing concentration of poverty among tribals who suffer from multiple deprivations is a matter of concern.

The percentage of ST population among the rural poor has been increasing fast. It increased from 14.8 in 1993-94 to 17.5 in 1999-2000. The increase was mainly on account of the comparatively slower reduction in the incidence of poverty among the STs. The percentage of poor among the STs declined from 50 in 1993-94 to 44.2 in 1999-2000 whereas for all rural population it declined from 37 to 27. Bihar, Gujarat, Madhya Pradesh and Maharashtra together accounted for 75.5 percent of the poor among STs in 1999-2000. It is noteworthy that nearly 30 percent of the poor were located in Madhya Pradesh. The poverty levels of STs in rural areas were high in Orissa (73 percent), Bihar (59 percent), Madhya Pradesh (57 percent), and West Bengal (50 percent) and in urban areas, in Orissa (59 percent), Karnataka (52 percent), Andhra Pradesh (46 percent), and Bihar (43 percent). Even in the 21st century the world is predominantly rural, especially the developing world. In spite of fast growing urbanization and industrialisation, a vast majority of people in the world development report 2000/2001 estimates, about 69 percent of the people of the low income countries live in rural settlements and in South Asia the figure stands at 72 percent.

Rural development has emerged as a distinct field of policy and research in the last three decades and is almost at the top of the agenda in national policies of the developing countries of Asia, Africa and Latin America.

Poverty alleviation has been one of the guiding principles of the planning process in India. The role of economic growth in providing more employment avenues to the population has been recognized. The growth-oriented approach has been reinforced by focusing on specific sectors which provide greater process. The various dimensions of poverty relating to health, education and their basic services have been progressively internalised in the planning process. Central and state governments have considerably enhanced allocations for the provision of education, health, sanitation and other facilities which promote capacity-building and well-being of the poor. Investments in agriculture, area development programmes and afforestation provide avenues for employment and income. Special programmes have been taken up for the welfare of schedule castes (SCs) and scheduled tribes (STs), the disabled and other vulnerable groups. Anti-poverty programmes that seek to transfer assets and skills to people for self-employment coupled with public works programmes that enable people to cope up with transient poverty, are the third strand of larger anti-poverty strategy. The targeted public distribution system (tdps) protects the poor from the adverse effects of a rise in prices and ensures food and nutrition security at affordable prices. Our efforts at reducing poverty are less effective. Despite completion of many anti-poverty programmes, there is no commensurate decline in poverty. The incidence of income poverty has declined from about 36 percent in the early nineties to some where around 25-30 percent but yet the pick-up in growth has not translated into a commensurate decline in poverty. India continues the low ranking of 127 in 2005 also in human development index (HDI).

As far as income poverty is concerned, the Planning Commission (1987-88) estimated that 29.9 percent live below the poverty line, out of which 33.4 percent in rural areas and 20.1 percent in urban areas. However, the World Bank report has envisaged that although the poverty rate has declined in

TABLE 5

Estimates of Poverty

Year	Poverty Ratio (Percent)			Number of Poor (Million)		
	Rural	Urban	Combined	Rural	Urban	Combined
1973-74	56.4	49	54.9	261.3	60	321.3
1977-78	53.1	45	51.3	264.3	64.6	328.9
1983	45.7	40.8	44.5	252	70.9	322.9
1987-88	39.1	38.2	38.6	231.9	75.2	307.1
1993-94	37.3	32.4	36	244	76.3	320.3
1999-00	27.1	23.6	26.1	193.2	67.1	260.3
2007 (target)	21.1	15.1	19.3	—	—	—

Source: Economic Survey 2003-04 and Planning Commission.

India, yet the actual number of people living in poverty continued that the country has more than 320 million adject poor people unable to muster an income equivalent to the $1 a day needed to buy basic foods. It has also been further depicted in the report that "the poverty imposes an oppressive weight on India, especially in the rural areas, where almost three out of four Indian and 77 percent of poor live."

The rural-urban gaps in the poverty estimates are also of interest. Looking first at the base year (1987-88), the rural-urban gap based on adjusted estimates is much larger than that based on official estimates. Indeed, the latter suggest no difference between rural and urban poverty in that year. This is hard to reconcile with independent evidence on living conditions in rural and urban areas, such as a life-expectancy gap of about seven years in favour of urban areas around that time. The incident of poverty is high among the Scheduled Castes, Schedule Tribes, landless general castes, backward caste laborers, petty vendors, marginal farmers, landless women headed households and dalit minorities.

INCIDENCE OF RURAL POVERTY IN INDIA

In fact, poverty of the worst kind was seen in the institution of slavery in India. It has been recorded that

TABLE 6

Percentage Distribution of Persons Below Poverty Line by Occupation Groups-Statewise, 1993-94 and 1999-2000

(Rural)

State	*Year*	*Arti-sans*	*Agricul-tural Labour*	*Non-Agricul-ture Labour*	*Self-employed in Agriculture*	*Others*	*Total*
Andhra	1993-94	7.8	51.3	7.3	19.2	14.3	100
Pradesh	1999-00	10.5	63.9	4.6	18.5	2.5	
Assam	1993-94	9.6	28.7	15.5	40.2	6.0	100
	1999-00	15.2	27.8	20.6	28.6	7.8	
Bihar	1993-94	11.0	46.9	3.7	32.2	6.3	100
	1999-00	12.3	46.5	6.3	26.4	8.5	
Gujarat	1993-94	7.6	49.2	9.1	18.8	15.3	100
	1999-00	7.1	59.1	10.8	19.1	3.8	
Haryana	1993-94	14.3	32.1	18.8	29.4	5.4	100
	1999-00	17.2	5.3	22.2	6.6	3.9	
Himachal	1993-94	7.9	4.3	17.6	65.8	4.4	100
Pradesh	1999-00	12.5	8.0	34.1	40.6	4.8	
Karnataka	1993-94	12.6	54.2	2.9	28.5	1.8	100
	1999-00	8.8	59.7	4.2	24.7	2.7	
Kerala	1993-94	13.3	35.0	23.2	11.2	17.3	100
	1999-00	14.6	46.7	25.4	7.6	5.8	
Madhya	1993-94	5.2	45.2	4.8	42.8	1.9	100
Pradesh	1999-00	6.2	51.2	6.1	34.0	2.4	
Maharashtra	1993-94	5.1	48.9	6.6	19.1	20.4	100
	1999-00	5.5	66.4	4.1	20.6	3.3	
Orissa	1993-94	14.2	45.2	5.3	30.8	4.4	100
	1999-00	8.2	55.9	4.2	26.6	5.1	
Punjab	1993-94	12.4	64.3	11.2	7.7	4.4	100
	1999-00	11.1	66.0	10.5	5.2	7.1	
Rajasthan	1993-94	9.4	14.1	27.9	42.4	6.2	100
	1999-00	9.2	16.0	22.3	47.8	4.7	
Tamil Nadu	1993-94	8.2	61.4	9.5	16.0	4.8	100
	1999-00	10.0	65.5	9.5	9.7	5.4	
Uttar Pradesh	1993-94	14.0	26.5	6.0	49.5	3.9	100
	1999-00	17.2	29.9	6.9	40.1	5.9	
West Bengal	1993-94	18.3	44.1	13.7	21.5	2.5	100
	1999-00	20.4	55.4	5.5	15.4	3.1	
Other States	1993-94	9.6	21.1	16.8	43.6	8.9	100
and Union Territories	1999-00	3.2	33.2	13.5	38.7	11.4	
All India	1993-94	11.2	40.7	8.4	33.2	6.5	100
	1999-00	12.3	46.8	7.6	28.1	5.3	

Source Computed from NSS 50th Rounds Data on Household Consumer Expenditure.

TABLE 7

Percentage Distribution of Persons Below Poverty Line by Caste-Statewise, 1993-94 and 1999-2000

(Rural)

State	*Year*	*ST*	*SC*	*OBC*	*Others*	*Total*
Andhra	1993-94	15.4	31.6		53	100
Pradesh	1999-00	15.6	35.0	41.3	(49.4) 8.1	
Assam	1993-94	13.3	9.3		77.5	100
	1999-00	15.4	12.5	18.8	(72.1) 55.3	
Bihar	1993-94	10.1	26.5		63.4	100
	1999-00	9.5	28.1	5.04	(62.4) 12.0	
Gujarat	1993-94	30.8	18.0		51.1	100
	1999-00	43.1	13.8	29.3	(43.1) 13.8	
Haryana	1993-94	—	47.2		52.8	100
	1999-00	—	55.4	36.9	(44.6) 13.8	
Himachal	1993-94	9.2	79.1		61.7	100
Pradesh	1999-00	2.7	41.9	10.7	(55.4) 44.7	
Karnataka	1993-94	11.7	32.5		57	100
	1999-00	11.6	30.0	36.6	(58.8) 21.9	
Kerala	1993-94	2.2	14.9		81	100
	1999-00	4.5	16.4	59.3	(79.1) 19.8	
Madhya	1993-94	41.4	19.5		39	100
Pradesh	1999-00	42.9	16.0	36.0	(41.0) 5.0	
Maharashtra	1993-94	18.1	22.0		59.9	100
	1999-00	31.7	17.7	28.5	(50.6) 22.1	
Orissa	1993-94	36.0	18.5		45.5	100
	1999-00	4.11	22.4	26.4	(36.4) 10.0	
Punjab	1993-94	—	74.9		25.1	100
	1999-00	—	78.7	17.1	(21.4) 4.3	
Rajasthan	1993-94	28.8	26.4		44.5	100
	1999-00	36.5	23.7	27.5	(39.8) 12.3	
Tamil Nadu	1993-94	2.7	34.6		62.7	100
	1999-00	2.6	48.5	46.1	(48.8) 2.7	
Uttar Pradesh	1993-94	0.8	33.7		65.5	100
	1999-00	1.4	34.6	47.6	(64.1) 16.5	
West Bengal	1993-94	12.4	35.1		51.5	100
	1999-00	10.6	30.1	4.3	(59.3) 55.0	
Other States	1993-94	52.7	12.6		34.7	100
and Union Territories	1999-00	39.4	13.5	13.3	(47.1) 33.8	
All India	1993-94	14.8	27.6		57.6	100
	1999-00					

Note: Figures in parenthesis include OBC also.

Source: Computed from NSS 50th and 55th Rounds Data on Household Consumer Expenditure

slavery has a continuous component of the social and economic life of ancient India. Historical records in India prove that a vast majority of Indians were always in poverty and knew to no other than that of want and starvation.

The first economist who attempted to study poverty in India was Dadabhi Naoroji, who stated his views on Indian poverty in his book entitled 'Poverty in India', in the year 1988. After Dadabhai Naoroji, it was Gandhi who made a serious attempt to fathom the depth of Indian poverty and seriously thought of ways and means to ameliorate the

TABLE 8

Some Other Estimates of Poverty in India (Head Count Ratios)

NSS	*Year*	*Rural*			*Urban*		
		Dutt	*Gupta*	*S. Tendulkar*	*Dutt*	*Gupta*	*S. Tendulkar*
27	October 72-September 73	55.4	NA	57.2	45.7	NA	47.0
28	October 73-June 74	55.7	NA	56.2	48.0	NA	49.2
32	Jul 77-June 78	52.2	NA	54.5	40.5	NA	42.3
38	January-December 83	45.3	45.6	49.0	35.7	40.6	38.3
42	July 86-June 87	38.8	NA	45.2	34.3	NA	35.4
43	July 87-June 88	39.2	39.1	44.9	36.2	38.2	35.1
44	July 88-June 89	39.1	NA	42.2	36.6	NA	34.8
45	July 89-June 90	34.3	33.7	36.7	33.4	36.0	34.8
46	July 90-June 91	36.4	35.0	37.5	32.8	35.3	35.0
47	July 91-December 91	37.4	NA	40.1	33.2	NA	34.8
48	January 92- December 91	43.5	41.7	46.1	33.7	37.8	36.4
49	January 93-June 93	NA	NA	44.2	NA	NA	38.9
50	July 93-June 93	36.7	37.3	39.7	30.5	32.4	30.9
51	July 94-June 95	41.0	38.0	43.6	33.5	34.2	34.1
52	July 95-June 96	37.2	38.3	40.1	28.0	30.0	23.7
53	January 97-December 97	35.8	38.5	38.3	30.0	33.9	31.0
54	January 98-June 98	NA	45.3	44.9	NA	34.6	31.6

Abhijit Sen, "Estimates of Consumer Expenditure and its Distribution—Statistical priorities NSS 55th Round", *Economic and Political Weekly*, December 16, 2000, Table 1.

TABLE 9

Poverty Estimates Based on the 55th NSS Round (Year-1999-2000) (Percent)

Reference	*All India*	*Rural*	*Urban*
30 day recall	26.1	27.9	23.62
7 day recall	23.33	24.02	21.59

Source: Planning Commission, Results reproduced in Government of India, Ministry of Finance, Economic Survey, 2000-01, Table 10.5, p. 194.

TABLE 10

Percentage of Rural-Urban Population

Years	*Sector*	*Male*	*Female*	*Persons*	*% of Rural and Urban Population*
1951	Rural	153444642	145199739	298644381	82.71
	Urban	32083820	30359889	62443709	17.29
	Total	185528462	175559628	361088090	
1961	Rural	183504095	176794073	360298168	82.03
	Urban	42789106	36147497	78936603	17.97
	Total	226293201	212941570	439234771	
1971	Rural	225319943	213725732	439045675	80.09
	Urban	58729333	50384644	109113977	19.91
	Total	284049276	264110376	548159652	
1981	Rural	270910547	252956003	523866550	76.67
	Urban	82463913	76998634	159462547	23.33
	Total	353374460	329954637	683329097	
1991	Rural	324321614	304370062	628691676	74.29
	Urban	114908844	102702168	217611012	25.71
	Total	439230458	407072230	846302688	
2001	Rural	381141184	360519109	741660293	72.22
	Urban	150135894	135219060	285354954	27.78
	Total	531277078	495738169	1027015247	

TABLE 11

Male and Female Literacy Rates by Rural-Urban Division (In %)

Years	*Rural Male*	*Rural Female*	*Urban Male*	*Urban Female*	*Male*	*Female*
1951	19.02	4.87	45.6	22.33	27.1	8.86
1961	34.3	10.1	66.0	40.5	40.4	15.35
1971	48.6	15.5	69.8	48.8	45.96	21.97
1981	49.6	21.7	76.7	56.3	56.38	29.76
1991	57.9	30.6	81.1	64.0	64.13	39.29
2001	71.4	46.7	86.7	73.2	75.85	54.16

Source: Economic Survey, 2001-02, Economic Division, Ministry of Finance, Government of India.

distressing situation. Another important work in this area is of C.N. Vakil who published a book entitled 'Poverty and Planning' in 1963, and this study found out the reasons for poverty in India. Lack of adequate work for vast majority of the agricultural population during the off-season, the social system which made one person bear the burden of supporting a large family faulty educational system, etc. In 1962, the Governement of India appointed a study group to make a thorough study of poverty in India and prepared a report on it and the group estimated that a total of 59.4 percent of Indians were below the poverty line in 1960-61.

Although the above data shows the rates of literacy both of the rural and urban areas, despite rising figures of illiteracy much higher in rural women than in urban women.

CAUSES OF RURAL WOMEN BACKWARDNESS

The major causes of rural women's backwardness are:

* Illiteracy.
* Poverty in Rural Area.
* Child Marriage.
* Burden of Homely Works.
* Population Overloading.
* Lack of Natural and Human Resource in Rural Area.

* The Biased Vision of Society.
* Social Exploitation.
* Poor Health Rate.
* Least Health Care.
* Dowry System.

TABLE 12

Trends of CBR in India

Years	*CBR per 1000 population* *Rural*	*Urban*	*Combined*
1971	38.9	30.1	36.9
1976	35.8	28.4	34.9
1981	35.6	27.0	33.9
1986	34.2	27.1	32.6
1991	30.9	24.3	29.5
1996	29.3	21.6	27.5
2001	27.1	20.3	25.4
2002	26.6	19.9	25.0
2004	25.9	19.0	24.1

CHART 1

Rural-Urban Trends of CBR in India

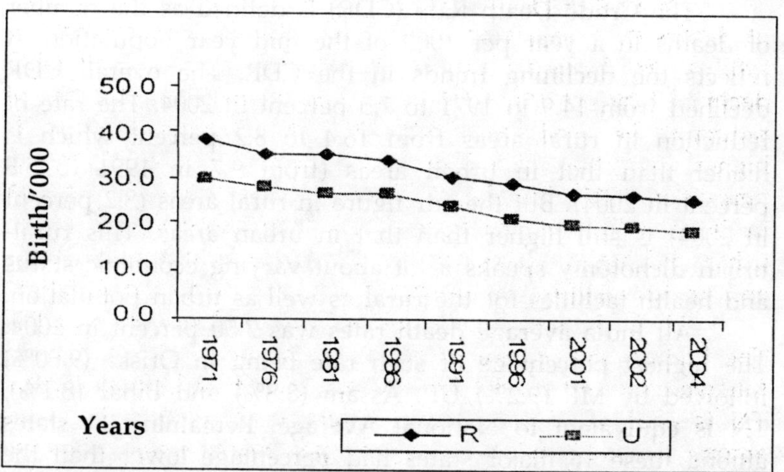

Source: SRS Bulletin, Various years.

Health Disparity in Rural and Urban Sectors: The following data shows the wide gap in the health measurement of rural and urban sectors.

Crude Birth Rate (CBR): Crude Birth Rate (CBR) means number of births in a year per thousand. In rural India crude birth rate (CBR) has always remained higher than the urban India.

In terms of Annual growth rates of CBR, its ranks in states had severe deviation from national average during the period of 1992-2004. In the said period states like Punjab, Himanchal Pradesh, Andhra Pradesh, Maharashtra and West Bengal fared well in reducing the cbr growth rates. But the picture of backward States like Bihar is very gloomy where reduction has been just less than 1 percent (32.30 in 1992 to 30.2 percent in 2004). Somehow this picture of Bihar reminds us of various factors like poverty, illiteracy, semi-feudal and unchanging nature of society and aversion to adopt new ideas and norms accoding to the changing needs of emerging era. It may be mentioned here, that most literate state Kerala stands at the rank one in terms of annual growth rate falling from 17 percent in 1992 to 15 percent in 2004.

CRUDE DEATH RATE (CDR)

The Crude Death Rate (CDR) is defined as the number of deaths in a year per 1000 of the mid year population. It reflects the declining trends in the CDR. The overall CDR declined from 14.9 in 1971 to 7.5 percent in 2004. The rate of reduction in rural areas from 16.4 to 8.2 percent which is higher than that in urban areas (from 9.7 in 1991 to 5.8 percent in 2004). But the cdr figure in rural areas (8.2 percent in 2004) is still higher than that in urban areas. This rural-urban dichotomy speaks a lot about varying economic status and health facilities for the rural as well as urban population.

All India average death rates was 7.50 percent in 2004. The highest percentage of such rate being in Orissa (9.60%) followed by MP (9.2%) UP, Assam (8.8%) and Bihar (8.1%), TN is equivalent to National Average. Remaining 11 states among these 16 major states had percentage lower than the national average. The inter-states variations are also

TABLE 13

Rural-Urban Trends of CDR in India during 1971-2004

Years	*CBR per 1000 population*		
	Rural	*Urban*	*Combined*
1971	16.4	9.7	14.9
1976	16.3	9.5	15.0
1981	13.7	7.8	12.5
1986	12.2	7.6	11.1
1991	10.6	7.1	9.8
1996	9.7	6.5	9.0
2001	9.1	6.3	8.4
2002	8.7	6.1	8.1
2004	8.2	5.8	7.5

Source: SRS Bulletin, Various years.

CHART 2

Rural-Urban Trends of IMR in India

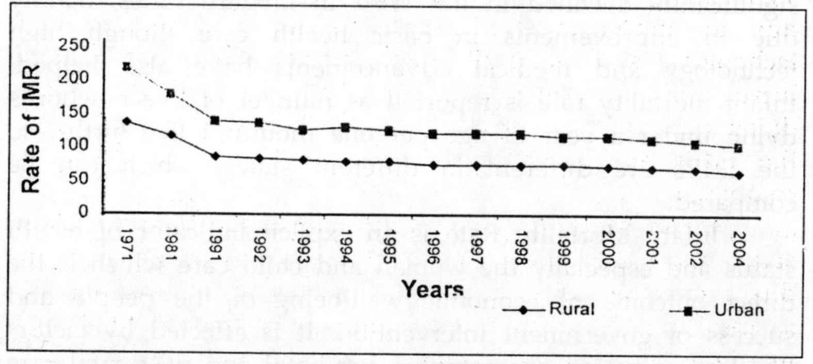

noticeable. Comparatively richer states have CDR below than the national average. Again the figure in Kerala is the lowest at 6.1 percent in 2004 whereas poorer states like Orissa, MP, UP, Assam and Bihar exceed the national average. Needless to say, these poorer states provide very poor health facilities to their population.

In terms of Annual growth rates of CDR, its ranks in states and deviation from national average during the period of 1992-2004 varies. Some States like Rajsthan, UP, MP and

Bihar had in better reducing the CDR growth rates during year 1992 to 2004. The CDR growth of Kerala, Punjab, Himachal Pradesh, Andhra Pradesh, Maharashtra and West Bengal are better than national average

INFANT MORTALITY RATE (IMR)

The infant mortality rate (IMR) is defined as the number of infant dying in a year per 1000 live births during the year. IMR was reported to be 79 per 1000 live births in 1991-92 and now it has reduced to 58 per 1000 live births in 2004. The main causes of death are disease of circulatory system, infections and parasitic diseases, injury, poisoning, pre-natal conditions, and diseases of respiratory sysem. The main constraints are low literacy and income levels, socio-cultural beliefs and practices, and suboptimal utilisation of health facilities. The infant mortality rate is also called the infant death rate. In the past, infant mortality claimed a considerable percentage of children born, but the rates have significantly declined in the West in modern times, mainly due to improvements in basic health care though high technology and medical advancements have also helped. Infant mortality rate is reported as number of live newborns dying under a year of age per one thousand live births, so the IMRs are different in different states, which can be compared.

Infant Mortality Rate is an explicit indicator of health status and especially the woman and child care which is the direct outcome of economic well-being of the people and success of government intervention. It is affected by factors like immunization programmes, pre-natal and post-natal care facilities for institutional delivery, etc. Poor people are more likely to live in massive over crowded areas without clean water and sanitation or in distant rural areas, also without clean water and sanitation. As a result, they have a larger propensity to have diarrhoea, cholera, or typhoid fever, (Martine, 2005). According to UN's Children Funds, diarrhoea is one of the three main causes of child mortality (the other two are malnutrition and respiratory infections) (Sachs, 2001).

Poor people are more likely to live far away from

TABLE 14

Infant Mortality Rate (Per thousand Live Births)

Years	*Rural*	*Urban*	*Combined*
1971	138	82	129
1981	119	62	110
1991	87	53	80
1992	85	53	79
1993	82	45	74
1994	80	52	74
1995	80	48	74
1996	77	46	72
1997	77	45	71
1998	77	45	72
1999	75	44	70
2000	74	44	68
2001	72	42	66
2002	69	40	64
2004	64	40	58

Source: *SRS Bulletin*, Registrar General of India, Various years

CHART 3

IMR Trends in India during 1971-2004

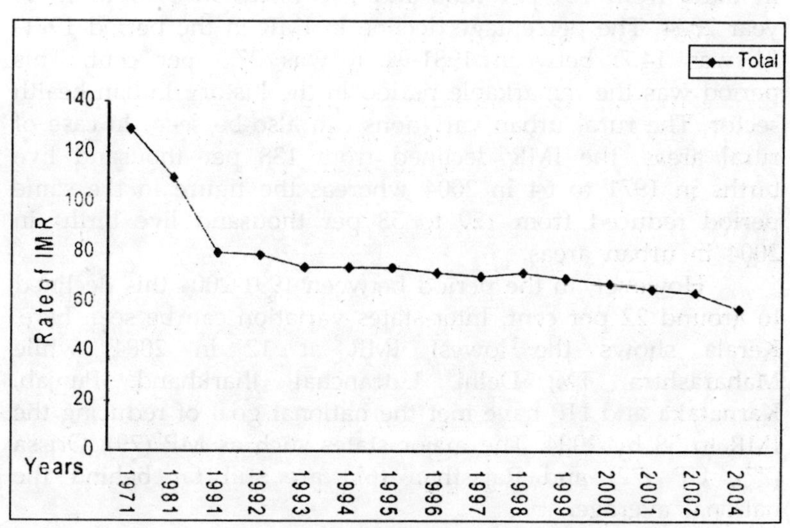

CHART 4

Rural-Urban Trends of IMR in India

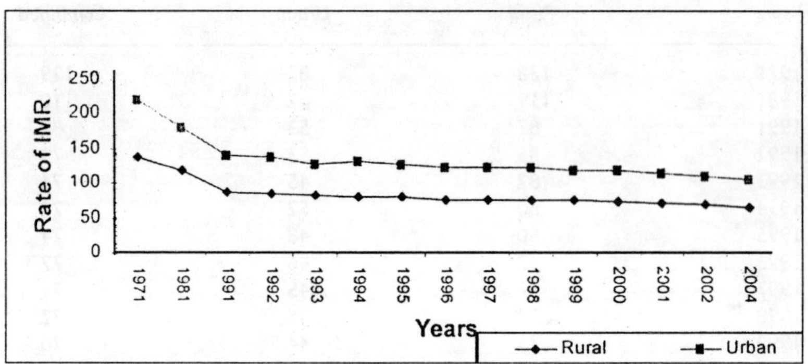

doctors and hospitals. They are more likely to have less education and hence understand the need to seek doctors or other kind of help. It has been widely docmented that one of the key determinants of child mortality in literacy of mothers. Educated mothers, for example, undrstand the need for hand washing, for the use of soap, for the need to drink of clean water. (Kiros and Hogan, 2001).

Here is declining trends during the last 35 years. IMR in India from 129 per thousand live births in 1971 to 58 in year 2004. The percentage decline in IMR in the period 1971-81 was 14.7; between 1981-91 it was 27.3 per cent. This period was the remarkable period in the history Indian health sector. The rural urban variations can also be seen. In case of rural areas, the IMR declined from 138 per thousand live births in 1971 to 64 in 2004 whereas the figure in the same period reduced from 129 to 58 per thousand live births in 2004 in urban areas.

However, in the period between 1991-2004 this declined to around 22 per cent. Inter-states variation can be seen here. Kerala shows the lowest IMR at 12 in 2004, while Maharashtra, TN, Delhi, Uttranchal, Jharkhand, Punjab, Karnataka and HP have met the national goal of reducing the IMR to 58 by 2004. The major states such as MP (79), Orissa (77), UP (72) and Rajasthan (67) are still far behind the national average.

THE GLOOMY FUTURE

The Indian market is very large and it is expanding by leaps and bound, but the retail shop-keepers of villages are being deprieved of their share in the retail market day by day. The policy of privatisation, liberalisation and globalisation has made the access/approach of the rural farmers in the market decreased. The rural poors are being poorer. The Computer and mobile has become not only important but essential commodities also. After all these commodities are beyond the approach of the rural people. The rural farmers are being labouress day-by-day. The holding of land is very small and there is fragmentation and sub-division of holdings. Thus the productivity becomes decreased. The peasants are living in worse condition in Karnataka, Andhra Pradesh, Maharashtra and Punjab. In previous ten years 1 lac 40 thousand farmers suicided. Employment and income avenues are being shrinked day-by-day due to globlisation policies.

The peasants of Vidarbh, Singur, Gharsana and Malwa are in restlessness. Their movement is against social and economic disparity and lack of opportunity of employment. Rural India is facing 'Crisis of Existence'. More than 400 'Special Economic Zones' are being created, which will destroy the villages, poors, farmers and their agriculture. In Ganganagar, Hanumangarh and Bikaner districts the prosperous farmers reserve the canal water in their grip with the linkage of malafide nexus of corrupt bureaucrats, whereas the poor farmers and their regions face the water scarcity.

The development of rural economy is linked with the base of social castes, religious systems and many orthodox practices which make the villagers unaware and ignorant towards their share/right/benefit in the economy. The 'Vicious circle of poverty' is very strong. The development of villages is possible only by eradicating those defects. The rural poors will themselves change the face of rural India and will decide their destiny.

References

Datt, G. and M. Ravallion (1998), "Why Have Some Indian States Done Better than Others at Reducing Rural Poverty?" *Economica*, Vol. 65, No. 1:17-38.

Hashim, S.R. (1999), "Employment and Poverty: Some Emerging Policy Issues", *A Quarterly Journal of the Indian Society of Labour Economics*, Vol. 42, No. 1.

Krishnan, I.N. (1992), "Population Poverty and Employment", *Economic and Political Weekly*, Nov. 14.

Mathur, A. (1998), "Employment, Equity and Growth", Presidential Address Delivered at the 39th Annual Conference of the Indian Society of Labour Economics at Thiruvanathapuram (Jan. 2).

Mehta, J. and S. Venkataman (2000), "Poverty Statistics: Bermicide's Feast", *Economic and Political Weekly*, Vol. 15, No. 35.

Minhas, B.S.L.R. Jain and S.D. Tendulkar (1991) "Declining Incidence of Poverty in the 1980s: Evidence versus Arts Facts", *Economic and Political Weekly*, Vol. 26, 1637-82.

National Sample Survey Organisation (2000). Report No. 455(55/10), Employment and Unemployment India, 1999-2000. Key Results, NSS 55th Round, July 1999-June 2000 (Dec.)

______(2001). Draft Report No. 458(55/10/2). Employment and Unemployment Situation in India, 1999-2000, Part I and II, NSS 55th Round July 1999-June 2 (Apr).

Palmer-Jones, R. and K. Sen (2001), "On India's Poverty Puzzles and Statistics of Poverty", *Economic and Political Weekly* (Jan. 20): 211-17.

Planning Commission of India (1993), Report of the Expert Group on Estimation of Proportion and Number of Poor, Perspective Planning Division, New Delhi.

Rao, C.H. Hanumantha and H. Linnemann (1996), Economic Reforms and Poverty Alleviation in India, Sage Publication, New Delhi,

Sen, A. (1996), "Economic Reforms, Employment and Poverty - Trends and Options", *Economic and Political Weekly*, Vol. 31 (Sept.): 2459-78.

Sethi, A.S. (2001),"Globalisation and the Emerging Pattern of Consumption Expenditure—The Indian Experience", *The Journal of Income and Wealth*, 23(2): 145-60.

———(2003), "Determinants of Poverty at the Global Level (With Special Reference to India", in the 86th Annual Conference Volume of the Indian Economic Association: 480-91.

———(2005a), "Poverty at the Global Level with Reference to India", in K. Nageswara Rao (ed), Poverty in India: Global and Regional Dimensions (New Delhi, Deep and Deep Publications Pvt. Ltd.): 3-23.

———(2005b), "Inter-Sectoral Linkages in Haryana's Income—A Temporal Analysis", *Artha Vijnana*, Vol. 45. Nos. 3-4: 147-60.

Sethi, A.S. and P.S. Raikhy (2002), "Economic Development and Poverty—An International Experience", *Anvesak*, 32(2): 27-37.

Sethi, A.S. and Ramanjeet Kumar (2001), "Employment Generation for Poverty Alleviation: Post- Liberalisation Regime Experience in India", Publication in the 84th, I.E.A. Conference Volume: 574-91, (Also included in Ashok Mathur and P.S. Raikhy (eds.), Economic Liberalisation and Its Implications for Employment (New Delhi, Deep and Deep Publications Pvt. Ltd.): 117-41.

Siegel, S. (1988), Non-Parametric Statistics for the Behaviroral Sciences, 2nd ed., McGraw Hill Book Company, New York.

Surya Naryana, Mill (2000), "How Real is the Decline in Rural-Poverty", *Economic and Political Weekly*, 35 (June 17th): 2129-40.

Tendulkar, S.D. and L.R. Jain (1995), "Economic Reform and Poverty", *Economic and Political Weekly*, Vol. 30, No. 23 (June 10): 1373-83.

World Bank (1997), Poverty Reduction and the World Bank, The World Bank Publications, Washingaton, D.C.

Thakur, R.N. (1998), Human Development, Economic Growth and Poverty, I.E.A. Conference Volume, Bangalore.

Thakur, R.N. (1999), Economic Reforms and Employment in India, I.E.A. Conference volume, Amritsar.

Thakur, R.N. (1997), Bihar's Development: On the Cross-Roads, Bihar Economic Rivival, Ed. A.K. Sinha.

Thakur, R.N. (1998), Education as Social Infrastructure in Bihar, *Bihar Economic Journal*, Economic Association of Bihar, Ed. A.K. Thakur.

Thakur, R.N. (1999), Infrastructure in Bihar: A Comparative Study, *Bihar Economic Journal*, Economic Association of Bihar, Ed. A.K. Thakur.

Thakur, R.N. (2000), A Study in the perspective of Socio-Economic Development in Bihar, *Bihar Economic Journal*, Ed. J. Prasad.

Thakur, R.N. (2000), Education and Political Status of Indian Women: A Key to Economic Development, Women and Economic Developments, Ed. A. Bajerjee and R.K. Sen, Deep and Deep Publisher, N. Delhi.

Thakur, R.N. (2000), Economic Reforms and Employment in India, Economic Reforms and Employment, Ed. P.D. Hajela and M.P. Goswami, Deep and Deep Publisher, N. Delhi.

Thakur, R.N. (2000), Amartya Sen on Human Development and Famine, Economics of Amartya Sen, Ed. A.K. Sinha and R.K. Sen, Deep and Deep Publisher, N. Delhi.

Thakur, R.N. (2000), The Economy of Jammu and Kashmir; Seeking Path of Development, I.E.A. Volume, Jammu, Special Lecture at University of Jammu.

Thakur, R.N. (2001), Tamil Nadu Economy; Marching Ahead, National and Sub National Economic Development, Ed. P.J. Gandhi, Deep and Deep Publisher, N. Delhi, Special Lecture at Vellore Institute of Technology, Vellore, (T.N.)

Thakur, R.N. (2002), Economic Reform and Employment Strategy, Technology and Employment, Ed. S. Murthy, RBSA Publisher, Jaipur.

Thakur, R.N. (2002), Infrastructure and Social Sector Development; A case study of Bihar, Infrastructure and Social Development, Ed. S. Murthy, R.B.S.A. Publisher, Jaipur.

Thakur, R.N. (2003), The Economy of Maharashtra; The Jumping Economy of India, I.E.A. Volume, Kolhapur, Special Lecture at Shivaji University, Kolhapur (Maharashtra).

Thakur, R.N. (2002), The Economy of Kerala; Human Development, Social Progress and Economic Crisis, I.E.A. Volume, Special Lecture, University of Trivendrum.

Thakur, R.N. (2004), The Economy of Uttar Pradesh; Bright Past and Gloomy Future, I.E.A. Volume, Special Lecture at B.H.U., Varanasi.

Thakur, R.N. (2002), For the Future of Prosperous Bihar, Souvenir, Economic Association of Bihar Conference, Samastipur College, Samastipur.

Thakur, R.N. (2005), Globalisation and Poverty, the World Panorama, Poverty Alleviation in the Third World, Ed. S.R. Singh, A.P.H. Publishing Crop, N. Delhi.

Thakur, R.N. (2003), Poverty; The Progeny of Progress, I.E.A. Conference Volume, Kolhapur.

Thakur, R.N. (2005), Poverty and Sustainable Development (Vol. I), Ed. R.K. Singh, Abhijit Publication, N. Delhi.

Thakur, R.N. (2005), Employment, Poverty and Development: During Economic Reforms, Economic Reforms in India, Ed. R.K. Singh, Nagaland University, Abhijit Publication, N. Delhi.

2

Inclusive Growth and Poverty in Bihar

BIRENDRA KUMAR JHA

"National prosperity is not inherited but created".

—Micheal Porter

Lord Mountbatten in his address to the constituent Assembly, August 15, 1947 said, "India will now attain a position of strength and influence and take its right place in the comity of nations" but his dream still needs to be realised. No doubt, following 1947 India made significant strides in multiple areas as it made a change from a dependent colony to a free democratic nation and the immediate challenge for the first government of Independent India was to accelerate the growth rate and this formed the cornerstone of the economic policies of Independent India. It is hoped that accelerating economic growth would result in the creation of employment opportunities and this would yield greater incomes and higher standards of living but it is also recently felt that accelerated growth must be inclusive for enabling the benefits of development to be shared equitably by all segments of society.

The Planning Commission which has prepared a document titled 'Towards Faster and More Inclusive Growth' aims to achieve socio-economic targets with an emphasis on reforms to attain double-digit growth during 2007-12 and for this, it lays emphasis on crucial sectors like agriculture, power, education, health and employment to achieve monitorable social targets in a time bound manner. After three decades of sluggish growth of about 3.5 per cent per annum in the post-independence period, the Indian economy attained an impressive growth rate of 5.6 per cent per annum during 1981-91 and 5.9 per cent per annum in the post-reform decade 1992-03 to 2002-03. Of course, the 1980s are now recognized as the period when India moved from the Hindu rate of growth to a higher growth trajectory. The broad social targets set for the 11th Plan are reducing poverty from 27.8 per cent in 2005-06 to 16.2 per cent in 2011-12, providing gainful employment to 70 million people, ensuring that all children go to school, raising literacy rates to 75 per cent and access to drinking water in all villages. It is also admitted that access to health services is in a bad shape particularly in rural areas and it needs to be boosted up. It is also desired to achieve 100 per cent access to elementary education by 2010 and functional literacy to be raised to 85 per cent by 2012. Undoubtedly, all these targets are in the direction of inclusive growth as it has been realised that economic growth has accelerated but it fails to be inclusive.

There is no denying the fact that it is not easy to say how much of poverty alleviation has taken place due to the programmes for poverty alleviation and how much due to economic growth itself. The importance of the overall economic growth as an enabling factor in poverty alleviation cannot be denied but it is now being increasingly realised that the growth process by itself needs not result in the eradication of poverty since the benefits of the growth may go to those sections of the society who are already well-off. On an average, at all India level, the average rate of poverty reduction was 1.14 per cent points per annum during the period 1973-74 to 1987-88, but it come. Down to 0.64 per cent points per annum in the next period 1987-88 points per annum in the next period 1987-88 to 2004-05, which is the period of higher growth (S.R. Hashim, 2007), supporting the fact that the impact of growth would depend more on the nature of growth and accompanying measures to reach the poor and raise their capability for taking advantage of the growth (Jha, B.K., 2007).

Despite all the good plans and programmes and reasonably good growth since early eighties poverty, one of the starkest manifestations of 'exclusiveness' has remained at unacceptably high levels although the percentages of population in poverty have, of course, declined from 55 in 1973-74 to 27.8 in 2005-06. It is but true that one of every three persons in India is poor, and two of the three are either malnourished or undernourished (K.X. Joseph, 2007). Although poverty has decreased some what it remains the biggest challenge to mankind as it has a de-humanising effect. It keeps people from realising their inherent human potential, forces them into unequal relationships that severely limit their freedom, exposes them almost defencelessly to predatory behaviour of others. Now-a-days, the more accepted thesis is that a reduction in inequality fosters economic growth, partly because of the effects on aggregate demand and investment. Many developing countries of the world are developing. The gap between the rich and the poor is increasing in the global era. Highly inegalitarian societies donot have good records of ensuring income security for their poorer citizens and sooner or later suffer adverse social developments that impinge on long term development or the sustainability of growth (Nagaraj, 2000). Poverty over the year has got more concentrated in fewer states and perhaps the most valid generalisation regarding the poor in a third world country like India is that they are disproportionately concentrated in the rural areas where they are primarily engaged in agriculture and associated activities. Undoubtedly, an extreme manifestation of poverty is inadequacy of food availability or say hunger which still existing in noticeable magnitude in some of the states although there is a significant improvement in the situation over the thirteen year period (1993-94 to 2006-07). West Bengal has the highest incidence of hunger (119 per thousand in 2004-05) and next are Orissa (61 per thousand), Assam (53 per thousand) Bihar

(28 per thousand), Kerala (25 per thousand), Madhya Pradesh (20 per Thousand) and Uttar Pradesh (17 per thousand). Hunger is concentrated among the most deprived sections of people mostly tribals and destitutes who remain mostly untouched by general programmes. Pullin B. Nayak (2006) has quoted a report from the hinterlands of estern Uttar Pradesh reports of the death of at least 12 moosahars who died of hunger over a 15 month span. Madhes Waran based on recent NSS employment round found that caste discrimination explained earning differences between the SC and the Non-SC/STs. While major differences in earning are due to human capital endowment, but about 15 per cent is also due to caste discrimination in market place. Findings lave shown that employment discrimination is substantial, especially in the private sector, and that discrimination occurs to a large extent on unequal access to jobs. It is worthnoting that the standard economic theory of discrimination indicates that economic discrimination generally generate consequences which adversely affect overall economic efficiency and thereby economic growth (Throat, 2007).

BIHAR SCENARIO

Home to approximately 8 per cent (8.29 crores as per 2001 census) of the total population of India and having approximately 3 per cent of the total geographical area of India, the state of Bihar is almost at the lowest rung of the developmental ladder and it is frequently characterized as the most backward state of India. The state has been ranked among the slowest growing regions of India. The growth of its gross domestic product (GDP) during the nineties had been very low, being just 2.69 per cent per annum from 1991-92 to 1997-98 as against approximately 6 per cent for all the major states of the country (Ahluwalia, 2000) and during the Tenth Plan (2002-07). The growth rate of its gross domestic product was 4.1 per cent against an average growth rate of 7 per cent for the Indian economy. The dominance of the agricultural sector in the state's economy is the main responsible factor for the volatile in the growth rate of Bihar's gross state domestic product during the 10th Plan.

Phenomenally very high magnitude of fluctuations in the annual growth rates, particularly in the case of agriculture where it has alternated between a positive and a negative growth rate, ranging from + 36.0 per cent per annum to –24.73 per cent per annum whereas even for registered manufacturing, which is generally much more stable than agriculture, the annual growth rate figures have varied between +93.93 per cent per annum and –41.44 per cent per annum. Hereby it is needless to say that the pace and pattern of growth, particularly that within the agricultural sector, exercise a profound influence on the level of poverty. Alakh N. Sharma and Asoka Mathur (2007) clarify the fact that under these circumstances, even when trend growth rate figures for a decade as a whole are high, for those engaged in segments which experience drop in annual growth rate figures to the negative range, the prospects of sudden slippage into poverty trap can indeed be daunting. Thus, fairly good trend growth rate figures by themselves can have little meaning for the poorer segments of the population, the bulk of whom are concentrated in the agricultural sector. However, despite these qualifying remarks, a good trend growth rate would be better for the poorer segments than a low growth rate.

If the econömics of Bihar and the country continue to grow at their respective 10th Plan rates during the 11th Plan period, the per capita income of Bihar in 2013-14 will be Rs. 1,5589 and India" would be Rs. 23,209. In this scenario, at the end of the decade, India's per capita income will be 4.15 times Bihar's per capita income and for bridging this gap a significant increase in the growth rate and a pattern of growth which can permeate its benefits to all sections of the society is desirable. In Bihar's context, the 11th Plan mantra is all-inclusive growth at an accelerated pace, accompained by improved delivery of social services.

During the 11th Plan an average growth rate close to 9 per cent with acceleration through the plan period to end with a rate of around 10 per cent has been projected by the planning commission and for Bihar the planning commission has projected four rates of growth of SDP at 7 per cent, 8.5 per cent 9 per cent and 10 per cent which may be possible

TABLE 1

Trends in Bihar's Gross State Domestic Product (Ninth and Tenth Plans)

Year	*State Domestic Product (Rs. in lakh)*	*Change over Previous Year (%)*	*Annual Average Growth Rate (Constant price-1993-94)*
1997-98	2592076	–3.85	3.25
1998-99	2788792	7.59	4.10
1999-00	2891397	3.68	4.03
2000-01	3450098	19.32	6.09
2001-02	3125936	–9.40	4.02
2002-03	3615961	15.68	5.25
2003-04(P)	3290950	–8.98	3.73
2004-05(Q)	3688196	12.07	4.46
2005-06(A)	3619819	–1.85	3.92

Note: P = Provisional, Q = Quick Estimate, A = Advanced Estimate.

TABLE 2

Growth in Income and GDP: Bihar *Vs.* India (Ninth and Tenth Plan)

	Ninth Plan		*Tenth Plan*		*According to Planning Commission 2002-03 to 2007*	
	India	*Bihar*	*India*	*Bihar*	*India*	*Bihar*
Per capita GDP Growth Rate	4.00	1.00	5.50	2.00	NA.	NA.
Growth in GDP of which:	5.50	2.90	7.00	4.01	6.45	5.67
a. Agriculture	2.00	–1.14	1.80	0.96	1.03	5.01
b. Industry	4.60	7.53	8.00	9.80	6.96	10.58
c. Services	8.10	6.37	8.90	5.08	8.64	5.12

TABLE 3

Alternative Investment Scenarios for the 11th Plan

Target rate of growth	7%	8.5%	9%	10%
Average Investment Rate	19.72%	23.65%	24.95%	27.52%
Public Investment as % of GSDP	6.90%	8.28%	8.73%	9.63%
Private investment as % of GDSP	12.82%	15.37%	16.22%	17.89%

only in different investment scenario from 19.72 per cent to 27.52 per cent.

For the low growth of Bihar's GSDP in comparison to the national average, the responsible factor is the low accumulation of physical capital recording abysmally low at 15 per cent of GSDP against 27 per cent investment rate for

TABLE 4

Trends in Rate of Investment

(% of GSDP)

Year	*Public*	*Private*	*Total*
1999-00	6.72	8.97	15.69
2000-01	5.28	8.79	14.07
2001-02	5.68	8.58	14.26
2002-03	4.70	8.94	15.64
2003-04	8.55	9.86	18.41

TABLE 5

Projected 11th Plan SDP at Alternative Growth Rate

(Rs. in Crore at 2006-07 price)

Year	*State Domestic Product*			
	7% rate	*8.5%*	*9%*	*10%*
2007-08	70784	71776	72107	72769
2008-09	75739	77877	78597	80046
2009-10	81041	84497	85671	88050
2010-11	86714	91679	93381	96855
2011-12	92784	99472	101785	106541

the country during 1999-2000 to 2003-04 along with lack of efficiency in the use of capital.

Although the Planning Commission projects a growth rate of 7.6 per cent, several arguments have been given in favour of feasibility of 8.5 per cent growth rate. Growth in the state will be based on the efficient use of existing potential and tapping into hitherto hidden potentials, especially in the primary sector. There is enough evidence to believe that the scope for increasing efficiency in certain sectors is very high, as many public sector projects are functioning far below capacity. A large stock of existing capital assets in publicly funded infrastructure like power, roads and irrigation have been lying idle for years and they need to be given priority for completing and upgrading as this would be more cost effective than undertaking new projects. Moreover, recent initiatives in institutional and policy reforms are yielding results, with private capital beginning to enter Bihar. The sectoral growth rates consistent with 8.5 per cent growth rate of GSDP during the 11th Plan period have been projected at 5 per cent for agriculture, 11 per cent for industry and 10 per cent for services although the planning commission expects 7 per cent agricultural growth rate and 8 per cent growth in industrial sector.

Undoubtedly, rapid growth has to be an essential part of the strategy since it is only in a rapidly growing economy that incomes of the majority of the population will be raised sufficiently to bring about a general improvement in living conditions. Bihar remains the third most populous state in the country after the formation of Jhakhand and the most worrisome fact is that about 40 per cent of the population is below the poverty line, which is the highest in the country. What to talk of Bihar, perhaps the most valid generalisation regarding the poor in India is that they are disproportionately concentrated in the rural areas and the rural poor have limited access to land and livestock, education, health care and well-paid jobs. Bihar where 9 out of every 10 persons live in village, their main source of income is agriculture and agricultural associated activities particularly agricultural wages or casual non-farms jobs. A large percentage of them are landless or near landless, the livestock they have is of poor stock, and are often denied opportunities for social reasons, such as caste, gender, religion, ethnicity and so, it requires an inclusive policy to overcome deprivation associated with all forms of exclusion.

Of course, for a state which is aiming at eradicating poverty for more than half a century, these are not to say the least comforting figures what may be, but unfortunately, we find lacking good signs in the post-reform period. And the most worrisome feature in the post reform period is the addition of the new poor among agricultural households in rural areas. We have a fairly good knowledge of the contours of what is called chronic poverty but apart from the chronically poor, a large number of non-poor households are vulnerable and they can easily slip into the category of the poor due to different types of shocks. The push can come from personal tragedy, e.g. disease and death of the earning member, loss of assets due to natural disasters, or loss of livelihood, or service impact on the current income due to market induced factors. If any of these factors persist for long a house with a thin asset base and without the advantage of a safety net would join the ranks of the chronic poor (M.S.

TABLE 6

Comparative Levels of Poverty in Bihar and India

(Persons below poverty line in lakh)

Year	Bihar			India			Bihar's share of poor in India (%)		
	Rural	*Urban*	*Total*	*Rural*	*Urban*	*Total*	*Rural*	*Urban*	*Total*
1983	417.7	44.35	462.05	2519.97	709.4	3228.97	16.58	6.25	14.31
	64.37%	47.33%	62.22%	45.65%	40.79%	44.48%			
1987-88	370.23	50.17	420.93	2318.79	751.69	3070.49	15.97	6.74	13.71
	53.63%	48.73%	52.12%	39.09%	38.20%	38.86%			
1993-94	450.86	42.49	493.35	2440.31	763.37	3203.68	18.48	5.57	14.40
	58.21%	34.50%	54.96%	37.27%	32.36%	35.97%			
1999-00	376.51	49.13	425.64	1932.43	670.07	2602.5	19.48	7.33	16.36
	44.30%	32.91%	42.60%	27.09%	23.62%	26.10%			

Source: Planning Commission, GOI, New Delhi.

Vyas, 2004). Moreover, with disappearance of local and regional markets, under the dispensation of the global market, small and medium size producers are unable to withstand the competition of the gigantic transnational. In this process millions of people are displaced from their place of occupations and habitats and are forced to join the ranks of the poor (Jha, B.K., 2006)

Despite all the good plans and programme for eradication of poverty in the state presents the fact that a sizeable proportion of the rural poor had never been covered under any of the programmes. As reported by a survey based study of sample villages and households in 1998 (A.N. Sharma *et al.*, 2000) 5.2 per cent of the households had benefited during the five years immediately under IRDP proceeding the survey. However, the percentage of beneficiary house holds and average size of benefits appeared to be biased against the poor. Not only higher percentage of households from big peasant and landlord classes benefited under the scheme but also the average size of the benefits were higher for these classes Beneficiaries were forced to buy poor quality of assets (animals in bad health or pumpsets which were non-functional), had to pay bribes and later return loans, and hence in a sense were worse off. Only about 1.6 of households benefited from JRY. Tarageting of beneficiaries was relatively better in case of JRY. Although JRY was found to be a better received programme, the works undertaken in the programme were inadequate and meager, resulting in generating little employment. In a number of cases, the project undertaken by JRY was abandoned owing to bureaucratic problems and malpractices. Housing programme was also a popular programme, but heavy bribes had to be given, resulting inadequate funds left for making houses. In respect of the anti-poverty programmes in general, the villagers often had to depend on some middlemen for taking the benefits of an of the government programmes. They had to pay bribes for getting the schemes sanctioned. The people saw government functionaries as inaccessible, inefficient and corrupt (S.R. Hashim, 2007).

HOW ANY GROWTH WILL ENSURE INCLUSIVENESS

The statement, "it is also true that economic growth has failed to be sufficiently inclusive" (para 1:2) reveals an acknowledgement of a concern that is not only expressed by the conventional critics of macroeconomic policies, but also reflects the dominant analysis of the current political paradigm, as expressed in what are called mainstream forums, such as the recent World Economic Forum (WEF) in Davos, by Klaus Schwab, the Executive Chairman and Founder of WEF as "The increasing distance between the rich and the poor" or high profile books by Joseph Stigliz, and the lecture on our Global Civilisation by Amartya Sen or the statement expressed by the Prime Minister in his speech at the Satyagraha Conference, held in New Delhi, Jan. 2007, "We need a new development paradigm that caters to everyone's need and can keep in check human greed" (Quoted by Devaki Jain, 2007)

Undeoubtedly, We need faster growth because, at our level of incomes, there can be no doubt that we must expand the production base of the economy if we want to provide broad-based improvement in the material conditions of living of our population, and if we are to meet effectively the rising aspirations of our youth but growth alone is not enough if it does not produce a flow of benefits that is sufficiently widespread and so there is a need for a growth process that is much more inclusive, a growth process that raises income of the poor to bring about a much faster reduction in poverty, a growth process which generates expansion in good quality employment and which also ensures access to essential services such as health and education for all sections of the community. Inclusiveness may at first glance appear to be only a restatement of distributional objectives which have always been part of planning, most notably a commitment to reducing poverty. Poverty reduction is indeed important but the concept of inclusiveness goes beyond the narrow objective of poverty reduction. It encompasses a much broader approach to distributional objectives. Distributional objectives are not viewed as an add on to dominantly growth oriented strategy. Rather inclusiveness is an integral part of the growth strategy and indeed the structure of growth sought to be achieved is likely one which is most likely to achieve inclusiveness. The multi-dimensional nature of our social objectives are reflected in the adoption of multiple targets covering not only growth but also poverty reduction in drop out rates, reduction in gender gaps in schooling and literacy, reduction in infant mortality rates and maternal mortality rates etc (Montek S. Ahluwalia)

Regaining agricultural dynamism, reversing deceleration in agricultural growth and thereby addressing the problem of rural distress may be considered as obviously critical for inclusiveness. In the existing institutional setup of Bihar, agriculture continues to be exploitative and dominated by its caste-class character, which determines the land ownership pattern. Over the years, however, changes have been taking place in the nature of class-caste identities. On the one hand, the upper caste landlord class has been selling off land mostly to the middle class peasantry belonging to intermediate backward caste, particularly kurmies, koeries and the yadavas. Institutional credit is also being cornered in a large measure by these intermediate castes. On the other hand, the backward castes which form the bulk of those owning non-viable tiny farms, often of less than one acre, have little option other than selling off their land and joining the ranks of landless agricultural labourers. A good many of these have been migrating in order to search for better economic opportunities, very often outside the state to destinations generally located in northern India. Combined with agricultural sector, these socio-economic forces have apparently been important contributory factors behind a visible decline in the proportion of rural poor revealed by the 1999-2000 Planning Commission estimates of poverty (A.N. Sharma and Ashoka Mathur, 2007). In Bihar agriculture has not benefited from the Green Revolution that ushered in a significant increase in productivity in several states in the country and so there is need felt for accepting strategy to increase crop productivity, maintain soil health, enhance produce quality and strengthen the existing marketing chain. The 11th Plan calls for corrective action in several dimension of agriculture. As suggested by former President A.P.J. Abdul

Kalam in his address to the Bihar legislature, the state can be the zone for a second Green Revolution in the country.

Employment generation is another priority area of concern. Given the unfavourable land man ratio and high population pressure in Bihar, the present employment situation in the state is far from satisfactory. The state is characterised by high unemployment/under employment on the one hand and on the other, low productivity of those who are already employed. An analysis of the NSSO data on employment-unemployment would reveal that unemployment rate in Bihar had increased from 6.34 per cent in 1993-94 to 7.32 per cent in 1999-2000. The estimated number of unemployed persons (by current daily status) in Bihar had in 1999-2000 was of the order of 23.97 lakh, of which 20.33 lakh persons belonged to rural areas, constituting 84.81 per cent of the total unemployment and so the objective of inclusive growth in the 11th Plan will require that sufficient number of jobs are created both in the rural and urban areas to absorb the number of new entrants in the workforce. Because of lack of adequate employment opportunities, the state has witnessed unprecedented scale of out-migration of labour force to different parts of the country. And so the following objectives of inclusive growth in the 11th Plan have been decided.

- Number of additional jobs likely to be created in the 11th Plan—49.37 lakh.
- Simplify labour laws so as to bring in flexibility in their applications for improving competitiveness of the manufacturing sector.
- Strengthen, upgrade and modernize institution for youth training.
- Enforce the child labour policy and policies relating to social security.
- Design curricular and syllabi to include technology and related areas.
- Encourage private sector participation in training and upgradation of training schemes.

Thus, policies relating to labour and employment will

focus on ensuring minimum wages, reduction of disguised unemployment, abolition of child labour, elimination of gender inequality and upgrading skills through periodic training, among other things. Social security and safety measures for labour will be given due emphasis. The age structure of our population is such that the proportion of our active labour force will continue to rise at a rate when most industrialised countries, and even China, face an increasing dependency ratio. This is an asset we must take full advantage of. This is a boon if we can create an environment which ensures skill upgradation and encourages investment in labour intensive manufacturing processes. It will become, however a bane if we fail on these counts (Man Mohan Singh, 2007)

The education and skill development is the greatest equalizer and therefore, the key to ensuring inclusiveness but unfortunately, education in Bihar has been almost stagnant, except some activities in the area of primary education, owing largely to the centrally sponsored scheme of Sarva Shiksha Abhiyan. The Mid-Day Meal Scheme (MDMS) can be an effective instrument for increasing attendance and also for improving the nutritional status of our children but much more needs to be done to cheek large-scale education migration of youth from Bihar. Educational indicators for Bihar have been abysmally low as compared to the national average. For instance, the gross enrolment ration (GER) for the year 2003-04 in the case of children in the age group of 6-14, who have a fundamental right to access free and compulsory education, was 56 as compared to the national average of 85 with a gender gap, the GER for boys being 62 and for girls 49, while it was 88 and 81 respectively for the country as a whole. The situation in respect of dropout rates is equally bad. Out of hundred children 59 donot complete grade V and 78 fail to reach grade VIII, the national figure of the dropout at the two stages are 31 and 52 percent respectively. During the last three decades literacy in Bihar has grown at sluggish pace in comparison to that of India. In fact, the growth trends in India during the last decade of the last century receive a major push upward as the percentage of literates jumped from 42.9 per cent to 65.2 registering nearly 22 per cent point change. On the other extreme, Bihar experienced a most increase of 10 per cent points from 34.5 per cent in 1991 to 47.5 per cent in 2001. As a consequence, disparity between India and Bihar that was less than 5 per cent points in 1991, has widened to over 17 per cent points in 2001. For promoting inclusive growth the government has envisioned its task as under:

- Secure fundamental right to free and compulsory education of equitable quality to all children.
- Stress on increased opportunity for access and skill building at the secondary and senior secondary stage.
- Appoint 1200 additional teachers every year to take into accounts the increasing number of children, leave and training reserves. Maintain the ratio and more towards the reduction to 1:30 by the end of 12th Plan.
- MDM to be extended to upper primary school children.
- Programme being launched soon to provide uniform to all children up to age 11 and to girls 14. The coverage to continue and expand.
- 15,000 new primary schools being opened by March, 2007 and 10,000 additional schools to be opened in the first year of the 11th Plan.
- 1000 middle schools to be upgraded each year of the plan period to bring the number to the current national average.
- At least 200 schools to be upgraded each year of plan period to de-link intermediate education from degree college and university.
- The government has released over 4000 vacancies of teachers in the university and colleges. Additional positions may be required for expanding the access.
- Around 25 engineering and technical colleges be established so that migrating students need not go outside the state, and the process is reversed.
- Madarsa and Sanskrit Board schools are proposed

to be brought in the mainstream and the Saman School Pranali Ayog is looking into this.

- Around 200 senior secondary school with vocational facilities will be opened in every year of the 11th Plan.
- A scheme to provide bicycles to girls in secondary schools is proposed to help them cover long distance. This would increase girls participation in secondary education.

Thus, action has already begun in the extra education sector to realise the objective of inclusive growth. The state government has constituted a group to chalk out a plan for schooling and rehabitation of children on streets and platforms. The report submitted by the group suggests that a strong common school system would be required for children with addresses, so that they access the neighbourhood schools without discrimination. However, for children who donot have parents/guardians/addresses, children home would have to be strengthened substantially. A large group of appropriate age children may be admitted to neighbourhood schools. However, those in the overage and adolescent category, some special schemes may have to be designed.

As experience of half century of economic development has brought to surface the exclusionary character of Indian society and its consequence for excluded groups, the alternative ways of overcoming the deprivation are suggested by the Social Scientists engaged in the discussion, particularly in the context of issue of reservation in private sector and extension of reservation for OBC in educational institutions and similar demand by lower caste converted to Islam and christianity and certain religious minority group like Muslim. Two alternative set of remedies which can be grouped into strategy of social and economic empowerment and of equal opportunities emerged from the discussion (Sukhadeo Thorat, 2007). Woman face exclusion as a category of population but it varies depending on their caste class and religious background. The state government has taken, perhaps, right step in right direction through reserving seats for women as well as SC/ST/OBC at the panchayat levels or municipal level. The government is conscious for empowerment of unprivileged groups of the society. For inclusiveness strategies for development of SCs, STs and minorities have been thought to be adopted.

- Establish a state resource center for women and child development.
- Institute a scheme to provide residential facilities for widows.
- Provide identity cards for disabled persons.
- Set-up at least one residential high school in each district for boys and girls belonging to the SC, ST and OBC.
- Provide stipends for SC,ST students in ICSE/CBSE and other affiliated and recognised schools through the education fee card.
- Formulate scholarship and training programmes and schemes for people with disabilities.
- Provide free travel concession for disabled persons in state owned transport corporation buses.
- Upgrade special school buildings for disadvantaged children and physically challenged people.
- Provide rehabilitaton to sex workers.
- Create a cell for the eradication of beggary.

Thus, for unprivileged class of the society several measures have to be taken.

The 11th Plan also commits itself to a greatly expanded public effort in area like health. With virtually no social health insurance and declining public health investment in the state, house holds have been left high and dry as out-of-pocket expenditure on health is one of the highest and this is leading to catastrophic illness, pulling down more and more people the poverty line. The commitment made under Millennium Development goals appears to be far away from reality given the backdrop of appalling health conditions prevailing in the state of Bihar. Health delivery in the state is not satisfactory. In 2003-04, full immunization in the state was 11 per cent against the national average of 54 per cent, the maternal mortality rate (MMR) was 452 per lakh live births against the national average of 407 ("National Family Welfare and Health Survey") and so improvements in health services provision are a priority as poor health services impact most adversely on the poor. Over the past few months, the government has initiated a number of reforms to resurrect the sagging public health system. With sustained effort, these hopefully rid the Health Care system of many of the serious drawbacks which had crept in, attention to which has already been drawn. The new initiatives in the sphere of health are essentially of five types:

- There are steps which have been introduced to make the Health Delivery System at the PHC as also District Referral Hospitals operationally effective by ensuring round—The clock availability of Doctors, complementary health personnel and adequate supply of over thirty types of medicines,
- The second major initiative is in the direction of improving the highly dilapidated Hospital and Dispensary infrastructure. Steps in this direction include repair and purchase of medical equipment, including electricity generators to overcome frequent power supply interruption, purchase of hospital beds and bedding, provision of telephone link to all PHCs and construction of essential hospital buildings.
- Strengthening of Immunization Programme.
- Women-oriented schemes for maternity care of those below the poverty line and appointment of female health workers (ASAA) for female and child care.
- The recent presentation made by the state government before the Investment Commission lays considerable emphasis upon involvement of private sector and Public-Private Partnership (PPP) so as to stop exodus of a large number of patients to move outside the state for treatment. While PPP is welcomed, this should not be at the cost of badly needed improvement in Public Health

Services. Moreover, in the case of private and PPP sector, it is important to bring them within the framework of a regulatory mechanism.

CONCLUDING REMARKS

The biggest challenge of Bihar as India's third most populous state, is to eliminate poverty, especially in the rural area and poverty can be reduced more effectively not only through programmes targeting the poor but through inclusive growth with a shift in employment to non form activities. This calls for an integrated strategy covering human resource development through improved access to education, health, drinking water sanitation, welfare and labour, and economic development through increased opportunities in industry agriculture, animal husbandry, irrigation, energy, Transport and telecom, supplemented with targeted programmes for the poor. The basic minimum needs can be most through wage employment, self-employment and rural housing. Therefore, the existing rural employment guarantee and watershed development schemes, Swaranjyanti Gram Swarozgar Yojana and Indira Avas Yojana would continue as thrust programmes for the elimination of hunger and deprivation. The poverty related MDG of halving the BPL percentage by 2015. This means that about 50 lakh rural families will need to be raised above the poverty line by 2015, i.e. about 16.7 lakh families during the Eleventh Plan or 3.3 lakh rural families per year. Assurming an elasticity of 0.4 between growth in GDP and fall in the BPL percentage, the target of 1.5 per cent reduction per year in rural BPL population required a GDP growth of about 4 per cent per year. The growth rate of agriculture is well below this. Thus, efforts will necessarily have to aim at faster non-farm sector growth along with strategies to rapidly increase agricultural productivity by focusing on horticulture, applying most recent remunerative techniques such as vermiculture, non-chemical pest management and other productivity-boosting practices, many of which are labour intensive. One thing more needs to be adopted is that programme guide lines. Should be revised to emphasize an orientation towards processes and outcomes, rather than targets as rural development is essentially process oriented and not a target-driven system. Above all, the efficacy of the 11th Plan strategies for inclusive growth would depend critically on the implementation machinery and so the delivery capability of field administration needs to be built up in different ways, including intensive capacity building good governance is highly desirable for achieving the goal of inclusive growth honestly and effectively. Economic growth would certainly help the poor but the pattern of that growth needs to be poor friendly. A large emphasis will necessarily have to be placed on those programmes and approaches which open the ways for independent and sustainable livelihood for the poor.

References

Sharma, Alakh N. and Mathur Ashok (2007), Transforming Bihar: Challenges and Opportunities in Global Meet for a Resurgent Bihar.

Hashim, S.R. (2007), Poverty and Inclusive Growth Memorial Lecture at 90th Annual Conf. of I.EA.

Singh, Man Mohan (2007), Agriculture, Education, Health and Infrastructure are priority Area in Yojana, April.

Montak, S. Ahluwalia (2007), Approach paper; Anything New 9 Yojana, April.

Thorat, Sukhadeo (2007), Labour Market Discrimination issues Related to Concept, Measurement, Forms and Reforms', Valedictory Address in the 49th Annual Conf. of ISLE

Jha, B.K. (2006), Employment Generation for Eradication of Rural Poverty of Post-reform Experience in India presented in National Seminar at Samastipur College, Samastipur.

Bihar: Approach to 11th Five Year Plan—Vision for Accelerated Inclusive Growth, *Kurushetra*.

3

Retarding Growth Prospects of Agriculture in Absence of Effective Institutional Reforms

D.M. DIWAKAR

INTRODUCTION

Every growth process has its political economy, i.e., science of class, which advocates its interest, protects its structure of property relation for production, exchange and distribution. Reforms in its structure, refers changes in property relations towards advance socio-economic order of property relations. In case of agriculture, institutional reforms refer to improvement in arrangements of property relations. Hence, institutional reforms in agriculture encompass transformation of economic relations. However, after abolition of Zamindari in the context of Indian agriculture, land reforms became synonymous to institutional reforms and unfortunately only redistribution of surplus land remained the core of the issues of institutional reforms. This paper is an attempt to understand institutional reforms in agriculture and examine a few select dimensions responsible for retarding growth prospects of the economy of Bihar. This paper has been divided in four parts. Part one deals with the framework of agrarian reforms. Part two discusses briefly about historical contours of institutional reforms in agriculture. Part three dwells into the issues of agrarian reforms in Bihar and part four analyses governance and finally summarizes the discussions and reflects on its implications.

I. CONCEPTUAL FRAMEWORK OF AGRARIAN REFORMS

Agrarian reforms as a process of development basically aimed at unleashing productive forces from agriculture across the globe to spread up growth rate of agriculture on the one hand and enhance the capabilities of poor towards human development on the other. This development Strategy emerged in the post-World War period. Many colonies achieved their political freedom and the aspirations of major anti-colonial forces mainly peasantry compelled their national government to enact and implement land reforms. Therefore, land reform measures appeared as State initiatives (from above) in consonance with peasant's aspirations. However, Occupational Forces (General Mac Arthur for example in Japan and Taiwan) were also forced to take active part in agrarian reforms to do away with feudal hurdles of agricultural development (Dorner, 1972:21; Joshi, 1982:36; Radhakrishnan, 1989:14). Thus, State initiatives were the outcomes of peasant struggles (from below). Transfer of land in this process from large holdings to petty holders as it was after independence in India or *vice-versa* in the corporate agriculture of developed countries and now in India also. Evidences from various countries suggest that France, Netherlands, China, Japan, Russia and many other countries could bring qualitative change in production relations and development process through land redistribution. It is also seen that land reforms provides savings out of conspicuous extravagant consumption and leakages of landlords. Tenants are liberated from illegal exaction and non-market coercion and constraints. This provides surplus to invest in agriculture to increase production and productivity and also works towards diversification of agriculture and non-agricultural activities and thereby changes occupational structure (Bagchi, 2000).

When land reforms emerged as one of the most important development strategies in the post-World War period, India was not an exception to this phenomenon. Needless to mention here that history of land reforms in different parts of the country was not a liberal gift from enlightened government rather it was an outcome of historical process necessitated by protracted peasant struggle (Radhakrishnan, 1989:13). It was an outcome of growing consciousness and realisation, irrespective of geographical boundaries and ideological variations, that agrarian reforms would unleash productive forces, enhance productivity, erode feudal struggle, address distributive justice and thereby contend resentment towards bringing a peaceful social order. India added yet another dimension along with peasant struggle, i.e. through peaceful mobilisation and persuasion– Bhoodan (Joshi, 1982: 88-89) however, it could neither sustain and nor achieve significance.

II. HISTORICAL CONTEXTS OF INSTITUTIONAL REFORMS

Creating institutions for revenue collection was probably the first step towards institutional reforms that Indian agriculture witnessed. Imposition of revenue farming as an institutional arrangement dates back to Mughal India, which was not only the root of inequality and poverty but also the seed of the growth of the Zamindar class (Tandon, *et. al.*, 1936: 2). Land revenue in Mughal India was fixed on the basis of produce and not on size of land area. It was not the rent but taxes, the burnt of which was felt by both lower and upper strata of the peasantry. However, upper strata had to pay less per unit of land than the lower strata. Moreover, intermediaries were authorized to collect excess over the fixed revenue to be paid to the king. Thus, there were inherent regressive tendencies to aggravate inequality between the rich and poor in the countryside (Raychaudhuri and Habib, 1982, Vol. I, Ch. IX, see also Ch. VII). This mechanism of revenue collection was further reinforced by the company government, which entered into agreement with Zamindars (Tandon, *et. al.*, 1936: 2-3). In this process small peasantries were subjected to exploitation which led to ejection of large section of small peasantry who lost their right of ownership on land and forced to be subordinated as tenants at will to Zamindars. Rampant exploitation of the peasants during colonial rule resulted into a series of peasant movements during national freedom struggle. Consequent upon peasant unrests in different parts of country, there was growing realisation during freedom struggle among national leaders that land reforms were necessary to initiate process of development in India. This was very much reflected in slogans of the movements (i.e., land to the tillers), the planning, legislation and enactment regarding abolition of the then land revenue system, abolition of Zamindari and intermediaries, etc. Basic documents that shaped their initiatives were Congress Agrarian Enquiry Committee Report, 1936, Congress Economic Programme Committee Report, 1948 and the Congress Agrarian Reform Committee, 1949, which is popularly known as Kumarappa Committee. However, Sampurnanand (1936) had better clarity than other leaders on these issues. He was of the view: "no radical improvement in the condition of peasantry is possible without the abolition of the Zamindari System." But he apprehended and warned a note of caution and emphasised: "We must take care, while eliminating one set of vested interests, not to create another set which might have equally hostile to our ultimate goal, viz. social ownership of the land and its produce" (p. xv).

In independent India, undoubtedly, abolition of Zamindari and intermediaries was a radical step to change agrarian relations. Concern of reducing disparity of ownership of land was very much recorded in Plan documents for structural reforms and agrarian efficiency (GoI, 1956, pp. 178-79). The First Five Year Plan introduced tenancy reforms and recommended occupancy right with certain subjectivity that ensured failures to provide security against tenants at will. Transfers were subjected to scrutiny during Second Plan. Provisions for verifications of transfers and voluntary surrenders were made operationally transparent in Third Plan. Tenancy was made non-resumable and likely permanent with exceptions in Fourth Plan. National Programme for Minimum Needs got such articulation in the Approach paper of the Fifth Five Year Plan. Approach Paper mentioned home-sites for rural landless under basic needs. Realisation was further deepened towards expansion of employment opportunities and minimum standard of living. "Even with expanded employment opportunities the poor will not be able, with their level of earnings, to buy themselves all the essential goods and services which should figure in their reasonable concept of a minimum standard of living. The measures for providing larger employment and incomes to the poorer sections will, therefore, have to be supplemented up to at least certain minimum standard, by social consumption and investment in the form of education, health, nutrition, drinking water, housing, communications and electricity" (GOI, 1973: 9). Thus, besides food, shelter and clothing, which were initially identified as basic needs, education, health, nutrition, drinking water, communication and electricity were added in the basic needs basket. Needless to emphasise that, these initiatives are necessary interventions. But the question arises whether these can be sustained without sustainable base for livelihood. It goes without saying that overcoming food insecurity and access to nutritious food, housing materials and clothes are by and large dependent on the produce of land and therefore, fulfilment of these basic needs is primarily dependent on access to land resources. Outlining strategies for fulfilment of Basic Need Approach to Fifth Five Year Plan document clearly mentioned: "Home-sites are as important as employment opportunities for ensuring to the rural landless a minimum standard of well-being. The problem can be dealt with most economically as part of land reform and consolidation of holdings. Home-sites for the landless may be treated as the first charge on any surplus land that theses measures yield. The surplus land may be transferred to an appropriate location by exchange and allotted as home sites to the landless" (GOI, 1973: 10). Thus, measures initiated by the government for redistribution of ceiling surplus and gram sabha land for housing, cultivation, fishing, plantation, pottery, etc., are pointers to examine whether these initiatives have been instrumental towards achieving sustainable basic needs through access to land resources.

First, Backward Class Commission was set-up on 29th January 1953 headed by Kaka Kalelkar. It submitted its report on March 30, 1955. This committee extensively recommended on land reforms and reorganization of rural economy. However, this report could not be placed for discussion before the Parliament. Backward Class Commission Report was submitted in 1980 headed by Sri B.N. Mundle. Among many other recommendations this Commission strongly recommended for effective land reforms.

"Until the stranglehold of the existing production relations is broken through radical land reforms, the abject dependence of under privileged on the dominant higher castes will continue indefinitely. In fact there is already a sizeable volume of legislation on the statute book to abolish zamindari, place ceiling on landholdings and distribute land to the landless. But in actual practice its implementation has been halting half-hearted and superficial" (GoI, 1980: 13.33, p. 60).

"It is the Commission's firm conviction that a radical transformation of the existing production relations is the most important single step that can be taken for the welfare and upliftment of all backward classes. Even if this is not possible in the industrial sector for various reasons, in the agricultural sector a change of this nature is both feasible and overdue." (GOI, 1980: 13.34, p. 60).

"The Commission, therefore strongly recommends that all the State Governments should be directed to enact and implement progressive land legislation so as to effect basic structural changes in the existing production relations in the countryside." (GOI, 1980: 13.35, p. 60).

"Apart from social traditions, the dominance by the top peasantry is exercised through recourse to informal bandage, which arises mainly through money lending, leasing out small plots of land and providing house-sites and dwelling space to poor peasants. As most of the functionaries of government are drawn from the top peasantry, the class and caste linkage between the functionaries of government and the top peasantry remain firm. This also tilts the socio-political balance in favour of the top peasantry and helps it in having its dominance over others." (Prasad, 1980, quoted in GOI, 1980, p. 60).

However, it is an open secret that Mandal Commission recommendations were reduced to the euphoria of caste polarisation and reservation on caste lines. None of the political force was interested in implementing unfinished agenda of land reforms. Undoubtedly caste polarisation made a dent against feudal ethos but suffered a setback lumping into the traditional identities. This proved a drag on unleashing productive forces from the stronghold of feudal remnants.

If enactment would have been the yardstick for commitment and realisation it was the largest body of legislation that India could pass after independence (Thorner, 1976: 18). But "there was apparent unwillingness of the rulers to do anything concrete about changing the production relations in Indian agriculture, which ensured that in most part of India even tenancy reforms and land ceiling laws, enacted in however diluted a form, would never be implemented" (Bagchi, 1988: 2). It is worth noting that the Mahalanobis Committee estimated 63 million acres surplus land adopting 20 acres per household basis in 1967. In 1970, government estimated 40 million acres, NSSO in 26th Round estimated only 12.2 million acres. Out of which government declared only 7.33 million acres as surplus.

III. AGRARIAN REFORMS IN BIHAR

In India, abolition of intermediary tenurial system was one of the major institutional reforms. However, this could not produce desired results. In select pockets, where peasant mobilisation was effective, land reforms could improve productivity and growth rates in agriculture and liberate tenants from illegal exaction, non-market coercion and bondage. Kerala and West Bengal could witness encouraging results. Kerala could protect civil, political and substantive freedom through egalitarian land reforms. Operation Barga in

West Bengal could improve the status of sharecropper and redistribution of land resulted into higher level of productivity and growth.. This led to better participation in education, health and development.

Bihar was one of the provinces, which enacted first Land Reforms Act 1950 and introduced Bill for imposition of ceiling on agricultural land in 1955, which was passed in 1959 and enacted in 1962. Ceiling Act was further modified in 1973 and power to take cognisance was transferred from the executive to judiciary since April 1973. Many other acts such as Bihar Act 1976, 1978, 1982, 1986, etc. were enacted and modified. However, ex-zamindars such as Darbhanga, Hathua, Dumraon, Ramgarh, Banaily, etc., and their near and dears could manipulate possible largest tract of land in their control.

So far official data are concerned, as tabled before the parliament by the Minister on August 19, 2004, about 4,15,447 acres declared ceiling surplus land in Bihar, out of which 3,90,752 acres were taken in possession and 3,06,964 acres were distributed. Thus, 94.1 per cent land declared ceiling surplus was taken in possession and 73.89 per cent land declared ceiling surplus was distributed. However, sizeable area of ceiling surplus land has been misappropriated through fake transfers and manipulations. Needless to mention that people's pressure with different political ideologies and shades through organised struggle could partially implement redistribution of land to poor people. Exceptionally sensitive bureaucrats played proactive role also but systemic limitations could not allow them beyond a limit. Land struggles by different people's organisations for redistribution of land and against fake transfers still continue despite state repressions and judicial patronage to landowners. Erstwhile evidences suggest that the beneficiary of land redistribution has located himself/herself in better socio-economic conditions and access to public credit institutions has been possible. Many of them have been liberated from bondage—formal and informal as well. However, in absence of follow up packages of institutional supports many of them could not sustain their land for cultivation (Mishra and Diwakar, 2005).

Agrarian Structure

Latest data available on distribution of ownership of holdings brought out by size of land in 61st round suggest that it is still quite unequal. About 80.7 per cent holdings is of marginal farmers. If small holdings are added it comes out to 91.7 per cent. About 6.5 per cent holdings are of medium cum large holdings. As per latest available agricultural census in case of Bihar, 80.2 per cent is of marginal holdings which have only 36.2 per cent of land area and 2.4 per cent large and medium holdings have 20.9 per cent land area. This is the situation of manipulated land records including fake transfers. Reality is quite different than records. Many times lists of surplus landholders have been produced before the Legislative Assembly but remained inconsequential. Tenancy market prevails with different terms and conditions to appropriate surplus (Diwakar, 2000).

IV. GOVERNANCE TOWARDS LAND REFORMS

Future programmes and agenda for governance that emerged through freedom struggle were *inter alia* land to the tillers, irrigation to every field, opportunity to work for every one who wants to work, etc. Gandhi categorically said that status of landlord would not be different than common people. Landlords would voluntarily depart themselves from the surplus land otherwise peasants would take away forcefully in which violence may take place. Hence, zamindars might cooperate by leaving away their land and state would play active role with minimum violence to ensure distributive justice. Surplus land should be confiscated without any compensation to zamindars. Various enactments of tenancy reforms since Bengal Tenancy Act of 1886 till date including abolition of the Zamindari System were significant landmarks. However, contrary to the later views of Gandhiji compensation package was ensured to zamindars. Implementation remained questioned, particularly after independence, as there was expectations attached with from so-called own government of the people of India.

Governance remained basic issues in the context of development in parliamentary democracy but unfortunately

Polantza's hypothesis was validated and governance remained confined to law and order towards serving the interest of ruling class. Loknayak Jaiprakash underlined this very categorically. He said: "The failure to implement those laws for such a protracted period of time has inevitably led to the growth of the rural violence that we are now witnessing. It is not the so-called naxlites who have fathered this violence, but those who have persistently defied and defeated the reform laws for the past so many years—be they politicians, administrators, landowners, or money lenders..... Also responsible are the course of law where the procedures and costs of justice have conspired to deny a fair deal to the weaker sections of our society." (JP, 1971:15). Even his own followers proved Kalecki's hypothesis right. Kalecki said: "Whenever social upheavals did enable representatives of lower middle class and rich peasantry to rise to power they invariably served the interest of the big business (often allied with the remnants of the feudal system)" (Kalecki, 1976: 30). If the Congress did not pursue land reforms, non-Congress governments in Bihar did not prove substantially different either.

Realisation of the implementation of land reforms in Bihar unfolds many dimensions, which were responsible for the failures (Yugandhar and Iyer, 1993). A senior bureaucrat very much in the helm of affairs of implementation of the land reforms, admits: "India is the only country where the judiciary has played a crucial role in frustrating and stultifying land reforms". (Appu, 1993:53). Another observation is quite revealing in the case of Bihar. "Bihar's dismal performance in the field of land reforms has been largely due to overhauling sway of large land holders over rural society and their dominant influence over the state's policies and administration. Moreover, the legal system is heavily tilted against the disadvantaged and there is lack of organisation on the part of potential beneficiaries." (Appu, 1993: 51). Whereas, critical review of the Task Force of Planning Commission adds a few specific factors for poor performance as "lack of requisite political will, absence of pressure from below, lack of effective administrative organisation, absence of up to date land records, protracted litigation and the writ jurisdiction of the High Court were creating legal hurdles" (Prasad, 1993:38). Even poverty eradication programmes proved a piecemeal for creating syndrome of dependence.

Failures of governance are very much reflected in anti poor delivery mechanism of the Government of India in general and Bihar in particular, irrespective of the regimes and leaderships to address the issues of the land reforms, minimum wage, poverty eradication programmes, development of agriculture at large specially in terms of land and water management along with facilitating support system, which gradually made poor disillusioned. As a result of continuous utter failure of governance in fulfilling the expectations, poor people kept on experimenting towards identification of forces of change. Many of them identified themselves with radical movements as alternative outlets for redressal. Instead of drawing lessons from the history landlords protected through state power remained aggressive and repressive against the interest of the poor. Agrarian violence in Bihar became unavoidable and the rise of private armies with a tacit support of the state made the situation of poor peasants even worse. Instead of expected strategies of supporting poor to promote distributive justice State generally took a position of governance in terms of mere law and order. Agriculture suffered a set back not only in terms releasing productive forces due to lack of productive investment but also betrayed the agenda of land to the tillers. However, Land Reforms Commission and Farmer Commission have been set-up in 2006. Their effectiveness to address the institutional constraints may decide the future direction of agricultural development. One may not expect radical reforms from this government also. Water management in Bihar is equally important for the development of agriculture. Unfortunately governance at this front has been an utter failure. On the one hand this indifference has resulted in drought and on the other hand it left agriculture in flood and water logging. Report of the Asian Development Bank 2007 underlines: "Flood affected about 30 million people in India—17.6 million in Bihar. In Bihar 13.3 million hectares of the crop and 255952 houses were damaged. The damage of public property has been valued at Rs. 74.3 million." (ADB, 2007). Agriculture with exception remained at the subsistence level insufficient to keep pace with the growing demands of agriculture and non-agriculture production system.

V. CONCLUSION

Agrarian reforms agenda has been kept at lower key through various agencies and mechanism, despite enthusiastic initiatives were taken up after independence. The gap between zamindari abolition and implementation of ceiling provided sufficient space for manipulation of land records, which has necessarily retarded the process of transformation of property relations towards advance mode of production. Hence unleashing of productive forces from agriculture remained blocked. Role of agriculture in reducing poverty could have been one of the best options in a resource poor states like Bihar, where effective land water management could have generated effective employment and income with relatively less capital intensity. But, measures of land reforms have been pushed back and now in the reverse gear and that of economic liberalisation have occupied the forefront. Priorities have been swayed in favour of non-poor initiatives in absence of political will. All these are the indicators of anti-poor governance which will necessarily lead to a wider social tensions and conflicts. Many of the radical initiatives of agrarian reforms were not taken up in the name apprehensions of disturbances of peace in the society and the society was kept boiling with growing intensities of conflicts and violence. There is hardly any doubt that the present ruling class in continuity of its predecessors will not work for radical transformation of the property relations in favour of poor. Thus, there is an imperative need of the hour that political will should be generated in favour of poor through the pressure of popular democratic mass mobilisations of the poor and their potential friends and catalysts and state should be forced to work in favour of poor. Otherwise, state will remain insensitive with contradictory policies for lip services to poor and will serve the interest of the ruling class.

Therefore, if the state is permitted to rule unbridled, growing marginalisation and disparities added with increasing social tensions and corresponding state repressions are going to be the order of the future of Bihar, where poor peasants will have less democratic space to raise their voice.

References

Asian Development Bank (2007), South Asia Flood Update, September.

Appu, P.S. (1993), A Modest Programme for Nineties, in Yugandhar, B.N. and Iyer, K. Gopal. (Eds.), *Land Reforms in India: Bihar—Institutional Constraints*, Vol. I, Sage Publication, New Delhi.

Bagchi, A.K. (1988), *Economy Society and Polity*, Oxford University Press.

Diwakar, D.M., (2000): Emerging Agrarian Relation in India: Micro Realities, Manak Publications Pvt. Ltd., New Delhi.

Dorner, P. (1972), *Land Reforms and Economic Development*, Penguin, Harmondsworth.

Government of India (1956), Second Five Year Plan, Planning Commission, New Delhi.

Government of India (1980), Report on the Backward Class Commission, Vol. I.

Government of India (1973), Approach to the Fifth Five Year Plan, 1974-79, Planning Commission, New Delhi.

Jayprakash Narayan (1971), Face to Face, Sarva Seva Sangh, Varanasi.

Joshi, P.C. (1982), *Land Reforms in India*, Allied Publishers, New Delhi.

Kalecki, Michal, (1976), Essays on Developing Economies, The Harvester Press.

Mishra, G.P. and D.M. Diwakar (2005), Land Reforms and Human Development, Manak Publications, Pvt. Ltd., New Delhi.

Prasad, P.H., (1980), Rising Middle Peasantry in North India, *Economic and Political Weekly*, Annual Number.

Prasad, Shankar, (1993), Implementation of Land Reforms Legislation in Bihar, in Yugandhar, B.N. and Iyer, K. Gopal (Eds.), *Land Reforms in India: Bihar—Institutional Constraints*, Vol. I, Sage Publication, New Delhi.

Radhakrishnan, P. (1989), *Peasant Struggles, Land Reforms and Social Change*, Sage Publications, New Delhi.

Raychoudhuri, R.C. and I. Habib (1982), *The Cambridge Economic History of India*, Vol. I, Orient Longmans.

Sampurnanand, B. (1936), *Agrarian Enquiry Committee Report*, Note of Ch. VI, p. XV.

Tandon, P.D. *et.al.*, (1936), *Congress Agrarian Enquiry Committee Report*, 1936, Prabhu Publications, Gurgaon (Haryana).

Thorner, D. (1976), *The Agrarian Prospects in India*, Allied Publishers Ltd., New Delhi.

Yugandhar, B.N. and Iyer, K. Gopal (Eds.), *Land Reforms in India: Bihar—Institutional Constraints*, Vol. I, Sage Publication, New Delhi.

4

Inclusive Growth in the Globalised India: Challenges and Options

G.M. BHAT AND SHABIR AHMAD PADDER

The approach paper of Eleventh Five Year Plan comes at a time when the Indian Economy has come on cross roads. There are inter-personal and inter-regional disparities. The differences across states have long been a cause of concern but increasingly there is a recognition of the problem of severe imbalances within states. Backward districts of otherwise well performing states, present a dismal picture of intra-state imbalance and neglect. There are gaps between different social groups in India, more glaring in case of SCs, STs and minorities. There are excluded groups in our society such as SCs, STs and OBCs and some minorities who continue to lag behind the rest. Another important divide in gender discrimination. The divide between urban and rural India has become a truism of our times.

The last three plans beginning from the 8th through the 10th Five Year Plan has seen tremendous economic growth under the New Economic Policy. But the economic growth has been mainly steered by the services sector followed by the manufacturing sector. The agricultural sector has seen large fluctuations and its average growth rate has been barely around 2 percent. It is notable that agricultural provides livelihood to around 60 percent of India's population. The New economic policy has remained confined mainly to urban areas and the rural areas have got a very miniscule share in development. It is in view of all these, the eleventh five year's main thrust is on inclusive growth. The Planning Commission approved the Approach paper to the Eleventh Five Year Plan (2007-12) on October 18, 2006. The Prime Minister, Dr Manmohan Singh, rooted for a growth rate of 10 percent in the final years of the Plan in order to be in "the front ranks of fast growing development countries". Presiding over the full Plan panel meet here, Dr Singh said that by ensuring inclusive growth, the Eleventh Plan would set "our economy on a growth path, which would finally liberate millions of our countrymen from the perennial scourges of poverty, ignorance and disease". What is implied in this recognition is that a sizable group of population has not been "included" in and have, therefore, not benefited from growth. Trickledown can take place if the poor are also included in the growth process that is they are engaged in economics activities that are growing, even though the non-poor may be the main actors and, therefore main beneficiaries of growth. When certain groups of people are not even 'included" in the growth process, there is no question of the benefits of growth "trickling-down" to them. Thus the notion of "trickledown" is not merely non-operational, it is irrelevant (Papola, 2007)

The approach paper to Eleventh Five Year Plan starts with the assertion that the Indian economy on the eve of the 11th Plan is in a much stronger position that it was a few years ago. After slowing down to an average growth rate of about 5.5% in the Ninth Plan period (1997-98 to 2001-02), it has accelerated in recent years and the average growth rate in the Tenth Plan period (2002-03 to 2006-07) is likely to be about 7%. This is below the Tenth Plan target of 8%, but it is the highest growth rate achieved in any plan period. While this performance reflects the strength of the economy in many areas, it is also true that large parts of our population are still to experience a decisive improvement in their standard of living. The percentage of the population below the poverty line is declining, but only at a modest pace. Far too many people still lack access to basic services such as health, education, clean drinking water and sanitation facilities without which they cannot be empowered to claim their share in the benefits of growth. These problems are more severe in some states than in others, and in general they are especially severe in rural areas.

INFRASTRUCTURAL DISPARITIES

The Eleventh Finance Commission devised an infrastructure index for the states for the year 1999. The index brings out a composite comparative profile of the availability of physical, social and institutional infrastructure in the states.

Amongst all the states that existed in 1999, Goa had the highest infrastructure index, i.e., it was the best placed state in terms of infrastructure facilities while Arunachal Pradesh had the lowest infrastructure index.

Disparities in the Growth of Gross State Domestic Product

TABLE I

Index of Social and Economic Infrastructure, 1991

(Arranged in Increasing Order)

Sl. No.	*States*	*Index*
1.	Arunachal Pradesh	69.71
2.	Jammu and Kashmir	71.46
3.	Tripura	74.87
4.	Manipur	75.39
5.	Meghalya	75.49
6.	Rajasthan	75.86
7.	Nagaland	76.14
8.	Madhya Pradesh	76.79
9.	Assam	77.72
10.	Orissa	81.00
11.	Bihar	81.33
12.	Mizoram	82.13

13.	Himachal Pradesh	95.03
14.	Uttar Pradesh	101.23
15.	Andhra Pradesh	103.30
16.	Karnataka	104.88
17.	Sikkim	108.99
18.	West Bengal	111.25
19.	Maharashtra	112.80
20.	Gujarat	124.31
21.	Haryanal	37.54
22.	Tamil Nadu	149.10
23.	Kerala	178.68
24.	Punjab	187.57
25.	Goa	200.57

Source: Eleventh Finance Commission Report, 2000

Mr Montek S. Ahluwalia, in his paper 'Economic Performance of the States in the Post-Reforms Period' has analysed the disparities in the growth performance of different states.

TABLE 2

Annual Rates of Growth of Gross State Domestic Product (SDP)

Sl. No.	*State*	*1980-81 to 1990-91 (% p.a.)*	*1991-92 to 1997-98 (% p.a.)*
1.	Bihar	4.66	2.69 ↓
2.	Rajasthan	6.60	6.54 ↓
3.	Uttar Pradesh	4.95	3.58 ↓
4.	Orissa	4.29	3.25 ↓
5.	Madhya Pradesh	4.56	6.17 ↑
6.	Andhra Pradesh	5.65	5.03 ↓
7.	Tamil Nadu	5.38	6.22 ↑
8.	Kerala	3.57	5.81 ↑
9.	Karnataka	5.29	5.29 –
10.	West Bengal	4.71	6.91 ↑
11.	Gujarat	5.08	9.57 ↑
12.	Haryana	6.43	5.02 ↓
13.	Maharashtra	6.02	8.01 ↑
14.	Punjab	5.32	4.71 ↓
	Combined SDP of 14 States	5.24	5.94 ↑

The accompanying table presents the estimated growth rates of SDP in the 14 major states in the pre-reform period 1980-81 to 1990-91 and in the post-reform period 1991-92 to 1997-98.

The following conclusions cań be drawn from the growth performance of the states.

1. The growth rate of the combined SDP of all the 14 states taken together has increased from 5.2 percent in the pre-reform period to 5.9 percent in the post-reform period.
2. The disparities between the performances of individuals states have increased significantly in the 1990s. The range of variation in the growth rate of SDP in the 1980s was from a low of 3.6 percent per year in Kerala to a high of 6.6 per cent in Rajasthan—a factor of less than two. In the 1990s the variation was much larger, from a low of 2.7 percent year in Bihar to a high of 9.6 percent for Gujarat—a factor exceeding 3.5.
3. The differences in performance across states become even more marked when we evaluate the performance in terms of growth rates of per capita SDP. The variation in growth rates in the 1980s ranged from a low of 2.1 per cent for Madhya Pradesh to a high of 4.0 for Rajasthan, a factor of 1:2. In the 1990s it ranged from a low of 1.1 percent year in Bihar and 1.2 percent in Uttar Pradesh, to a high of 7.6 percent per year in Gujarat, with Maharashtra coming next at 6.1 percent. The ratio between the lowest (Bihar) and the highest (Gujarat) is as much as 1:7.
4. In the 1990s while the growth accelerated for the economy as a whole, it actually decelerated sharply in Bihar, Uttar Pradesh and Orissa all of which had relatively low rates of growth to begin with and were also the poorest states. These three states together also account for over a third of the population of our country. There was also a deceleration in Haryana and Punjab, but the

deceleration was from relatively higher levels of growth in the 1980s, and these states were also the richest.

5. Six states of the country showed acceleration in growth of SDP in the 1990s. The acceleration was particularly marked in Maharashtra and Gujarat, both of which were among the richer states, but there was also an acceleration in West Bengal, Kerala, Tamil Nadu and Madhya Pradesh belonging to the middle group of states in terms of per capita SDP.
6. Another point to be noted is that the high growth performers in the 1990s were not concentrated in one part of the country. The six states with growth rates of SDP above 6 percent per year in the 1990s are fairly well-distributed regionally, i.e., Gujarat (9.6 percent) and Maharashtra (8.0 percent) in the west, West Bengal (6.9 percent) in the east, Tamil Nadu (6.2 percent) in the south and Madhya Pradesh (6.2 percent) and Rajasthan (6.5 percent) in the north.

An interesting feature of the performance in the 1990s is that the so-called grouping of BIMARU states (Bihar, Madhya Pradesh, Rajasthan and Uttar Pradesh) as poor performers does not hold true in case of economic performance. Though Bihar and Uttar Pradesh performed poorly, growing more slowly than the average, the other two members of this group, Rajasthan and Madhya Pradesh, have performed reasonably well. In the 1990s Rajasthan grew at a rate marginally lower than its average in 1980s, but nevertheless remained a strong performer. Madhya Pradesh's growth in the 1980s was below the average of the 14 states but it accelerated significantly in the 1990s.

Similarly, the perception that coastal states or the southern states have all done well in the period of liberalisation is not valid. Orissa being a coastal state has not done well whereas Rajasthan and Madhya Pradesh are heartland states and have performed reasonably well. The southern states as a group have done well, but they have not been the only beneficiaries of growth in the 1990s. In fact, Tamil Nadu is the only southern state in the top six best performers.

The performance of Kerala in the sphere of human development has been commendable. Its economic performance in the 1990s showed a marked improvement compared with the 1980s. Because of low population growth, its per capita income was more than the average for the 14 states.

In conclusion, the superior performance of Gujarat and Maharashtra must be attributed to the fact that the states were able to provide an environment most conducive to benefiting from the new policies of the 1990s. The key ingredients of success in these states should be identified and emulated by other states. Simultaneously the basic factors hindering the growth of the poor performers should be tackled at the earliest.

IMPLICATIONS OF INTER STATE INEQUALITY

Montek Singh Ahluwalia has estimated Gini coefficient measuring inter-State inequality for 18 years from 1980-81 to 1998-99. His estimates confirm the common perception that inter-State inequality in the decades of 1980s and 1990s has increased. Gini-coefficient measuring Inter-State inequality is 0.225 for 1997-98 as against 0.175 for 1989-90 and 0.152 in 1980-81. His estimates of Gini coefficient, measuring inter-State inequality for 18 years from 1980-81 to 1998-99 are reproduced in Table 3.

According to Montek Singh Ahluwalia, these estimates do not suggest that the rich States got richer and poor States got poorer. This inference is based on the following results:

1. Punjab and Haryana were the two richest States but their growth rates fell below the national average.
2. Performance of four middle income States West Bengal, Kerala, Tamil Nadu and Karnataka was above the national average. In fact, West Bengal registered very steady growth.

TABLE 3

Trends in Gini Coefficient Measuring Inter-State Inequality

1980-81	0.152
1981-82	0.152
1982-83	0.152
1983-84	0.151
1984-85	0.154
1985-86	0.159
1986-87	0.157
1987-88	0.161
1988-89	0.158
1989-90	0.175
1990-91	0.171
1991-92	0.175
1992-93	0.199
1993-94	0.207
1994-95	0.206
1995-96	0.230
1996-97	0.222
1997-98	0.235
1998-99	0.233

3. Bihar, Uttar Pradesh and Orissa the poorest States performed very poorly in the 1990s.

INCIDENCE OF POVERTY

Poverty in any society is considered an important indicator of economic backwardness. In India, poor are to be found everywhere, but the percentage of population below poverty line is not the same in the States. The Planning Commission's latest estimates of incidence of poverty in different States 1999-2000 are shown in Table 4.

According to the Planning Commission's estimates of the incidence of poverty around 26.1 per cent of the population of India was below the poverty line n 1999-2000. However, certain States, the incidence of poverty was much less. For instance, population below the poverty line was 6.2 per cent in Punjab, 15.8 per cent in Andhra Pradesh, 14.1 per cent in Gujarat, 8.7 per cent in Haryana and 12.7 per cent in

TABLE 4

Incidence of Poverty

State	1993-94 Poverty Ratio (Per cent)	1999-2000 Poverty Ratio (Per cent)
1. Andhra Pradesh	22.2	15.8
2. Assam	40.9	36.1
3. Bihar	55.0	42.6
4. Gujarat	24.2	14.1
5. Haryana	25.1	8.7
6. Himachal Pradesh	28.4	7.6
7. Karnataka	33.2	20.04
8. Kerala	25.4	12.7
9. Madhya Pradesh	42.5	37.4
10. Maharashtra	36.9	25.0
11. Orissa	48.6	47.2
12. Punjab	11.8	6.2 A
13. Rajasthan	27.4	15.3
14. Tamil Nadu	35.0	21.1
15. Uttar Pradesh	40.9	31.2
16. West Bengal	35.7	27.0
All-India	36.0	26.1

Source: Tata Services Ltd., Statistical Outline of India, 2005-06 (Mumbal, 2006), Table 166, p. 150.

Kerala. It is interesting to note that Andhra Pradesh and Kerala are middle income States and yet in these States incidence of poverty is far less than Maharashtra which is a high income State. As against this, incidence of poverty was as high as 42.6 per cent in Bihar, 47.2 per cent in Orissa, 37.4 per cent in Madhya Pradesh, 36.1 per cent in Assam and 31.2 per cent in Uttar Pradesh. Hence, in 1999-2000 out of 260.3 million poor in India, 135.2 million were in these five States. Bihar, Uttar Pradesh and Madhya Pradesh are big States. In 1999-2000, these three States together accounted for 42.0 per cent of the total number of poor in the country. This implies that there was concentration of poverty in economically backward big States.

DISPARITIES IN HUMAN RESOURCE DEVELOPMENT

Infant mortality rate and literacy rate are two very good indices of physical quality of life. Infant mortality rate shows a tendency to decline with economic and social development. From this point of view Kerala is far ahead of other States. In 2002 infant mortality rate in Kerala was 10 per 1,000 live births as against the national infant mortality rate of 63 per 1,000 live births. Punjab, Maharashtra, West Bengal and Tamil Nadu had infant mortality rates in the range of 44 to 51. The States registering high infant mortality rates in 2002 were Orissa (87), Madhya Pradesh (85), Uttar Pradesh (80), Rajasthan (78), Assam (70) and Haryana (62). Even on other criteria most of these States have been found to be extremely backward.

Literacy rate in general and female literacy rate in particular are regarded as good indicators of development. On these criteria Kerala (the first ranked State) has done extremely well *vis-a-vis* other States. According to 2001 census, the overall literacy rate in Kerala was 90.9 per cent, as against the national average of 65.4 per cent. Even the female literacy rate in Kerala was as high as 87.9 per cent. In the States of Bihar, Rajasthan and Uttar Pradesh the literacy rates ranged between 47.5 and 61.0 per cent. In these States the female literacy rate ranged from 33.8 to 44.3 per cent. Interestingly in Haryana, the third ranked State in terms of per capita income both overall literacy rate and the female literacy rate were more or less the same as all-India rates. This perhaps is due to the low priority given to education in patriarchal agrarian societies.

DISPARITIES IN INDUSTRIAL GROWTH

The initial distribution of industries in India was determined by the historical processes of growth in the interests of the British rulers. As a result, most of the industries got concentrated at a few centres. This pattern continued in the post-Independence period as well. For instance, a study of 28 large-scale manufacturing industries in India in 1950 showed the dominance of the Western region and West Bengal in the regional distribution of industries. Thus, 34.60 per cent of total productive capital was concentrated in Western region while 24.65 per cent was concentrated in West Bengal, their combined share being as much as 59.25 per cent. Taken together, the Western region and West Bengal accounted for 63.03 per cent of total persons employed, 60.41 per cent of gross ex-factory value of output, and 63.95 per cent of value added by manufacture.

This pattern of concentration has not changed substantially during the planning period despite all attempts made at regional dispersal of industries. For instance, as late as 2002-03 the two States of Maharashtra and Tamil Nadu accounted for 28.9 per cent of factory employment, 28.5 per cent of invested capital, 28.8 per cent of gross output and 29.1 per cent of value added by manufacture. If the three industrially advanced States of Maharashtra, Gujarat and Tamil Nadu are considered together, the true picture of regional concentration of industries is explicitly brought into prominence. In 2002-03 these three States together (having 20.4 per cent of total population according to 2001 census) accounted for 45.0 per cent of gross output, 42.4 per cent of value added, 45.7 per cent of total invested capital, and 37.9 per cent of employment in factory sector. The mere fact that more than two-fifths of the total output, value added and fixed capital and a little less than two-fifths of total employment in factory sector is found in these three States alone while the remaining States and Union Territories contribute only a little more than half of total value added and total output is a proof of substantial regional concentration of industries in the three industrially advanced States of Maharashtra, Gujarat and Tamil Nadu.

DISPARITIES IN AGRICULTURAL DEVELOPMENT

As far as the agricultural sector is concerned, regional disparities have increased over time with the States of Punjab and Haryana and parts of Uttar Pradesh pushing well ahead of others. This is due to the reason that the success of the programme of High Yielding Varieties of seeds (known as HYVP or New Agricultural Strategy) was largely limited to wheat growing areas. In fact, due to HYVP, the combined share of Punjab and Haryana in total output of foodgrains rose from 7.5 per cent in 1964-65 to 20.16 per cent in 2003-04 while these States account for a mere 4.4 per cent of the country's population (as per 2001 census). In 2002-03, per capita output of foodgrains was 964.3 kgs. in Punjab which was more than five and a half times the national per capita output (the national per capita output of foodgrains in 2002-03 being 169.3 kgs). The per capita output of foodgrains in Haryana was 583.4 kgs. which was about three and a half times the national per capita output. The position of these States *vis-a-vis* other States would be clear from the fact that the per capita output of foodgrains in Uttar Pradesh (which ranked third in 2002-03) was 218.4 kgs. and in West Bengal (which ranked fourth in 2002-03) was 193.6 kgs. Thus the per capita output of foodgrains in Punjab was more than four and a half times the per capita output in the third ranked State. The prosperity of agriculture in Punjab and Haryana is largely due to irrigation facilities and high fertiliser consumption per hectare of cropped area. In Punjab and Haryana, in 1999-2000 gross irrigated area as percentage of gross cropped area was 90.9 per cent and 85.0 per cent respectively, as against all India average of 40.2 per cent. Likewise, fertiliser consumption per hectare of cropped area was 184.0 kgs. in Punjab and 167.1 kgs. in Haryana in 2003-04, as against the national average of 89.8 kgs. in the same year.

SOME MAJOR CHALLENGES

Some of the major challenges in the 11th Five Year Plan's approach paper points out are:

(a) Providing Essential Public Services for the Poor

The most important challenge is how to provide essential public services such as education and health to large parts of our population who are denied these services at present.

(b) Regaining Agricultural Dynamism

One of the major challenges of the 11th Plan must be to

reverse the deceleration in agricultural growth from 3.2 per cent observed between 1980 and 1996-97 to a trend average of only 1.5 per cent subsequently. This deceleration is undoubtedly at the root of the problem of rural distress that has surfaced in many pats of the country. A second green revolution is urgently needed to raise the growth rate of agricultural GDP to around 4 per cent.

(c) Increasing Manufacturing Competitiveness

The manufacturing sector has also not grown as rapidly as might have been expected. The average growth rate of this sector has accelerated compared to the Ninth Plan but is unlikely to exceed 8 per cent in the 10th Plan. It should be targeted to grow at around 12 per cent or so if we want to achieve a GDP growth of between 8 and 9 per cent. The most important constraint in achieving a faster growth of manufacturing is the fact that infrastructure, consisting of roads, railway, ports, airports communication and electric power, is not up to the standards prevalent in our competitor countries. This must be substantially rectified within the next 5-10 years if our enterprises are to compete effectively.

(d) Developing Human Resource

To ensure a continuous and growing supply of quality investments in public sector institutions of higher learning combined with fundamental reforms of the curriculum and also service conditions to attract high quality faculty. The scope for expanding capacity through private sector initiatives in higher learning must also be fully exploited, while also ensuring that quality standards are not diluted. Unless this is done on an urgent basis, we will fail to attain global standards.

(e) Protecting the Environment

Environmental concerns are growing globally as well as within the country. Neglect of environmental considerations can lead to adverse effects very quickly. The threat of climate change also poses real challenge to the well-being of future generations which we can ill-afford to ignore. Our development a strategy has to be sensitive to these growing concerns and should ensure that these threats and trade-offs are appropriately evaluated.

References

Planning Commission (October 2006), Approach paper to the Eleventh Five Year Plan (2007-12), Government of India, New Delhi.

S. Mahendra Dev, "Regional Disparities in Poverty and Malnutrition, Paper presented at a Seminar at ISID, New Delhi, September 16-18, 2005.

Papola, T.S., Reducing Imbalances in Regional Development: An Essential Ingredient of Strategy for "Inclusive Growth". Inaugural address at the National Seminar on "Making Growth Inclusive with Special Reference to Imbalances in Regional Development", Department of Economics, University of Jammu, Jammu, 12-13 March, 2007.

Rajaram, K. and Singh, S.N., Indian Economy, Spectrum Books Pvt. Ltd., New Delhi, 2005.

Misra, S.K. and Puri, V.K., 2006, Economics of Development and Planning, Himalaya Publishing House, New Delhi.

Making Development Inclusive

An Introspection of Exclusionary Growth in India and Challenges for Inclusion

KUMAR RATNESH

PRELUDE

Making growth and development inclusive has become a challenge for planners and policy-makers in India at the outset of the Eleventh Plan particularly, when a majority of the ordinary people send a message in the 2004 general elections that they felt alienated from the benefits of remarkable growth performance of nearly 6.3 per cent p.a. during the last ten years (i.e. 1993-94 to 2004-05). Furthermore, the continuing high incidence of poverty and other form of deprivation as well as slowdown in agriculture resulting in despair and death of farmers has promoted the policy-makers and planners in India to advocate 'inclusive growth'. It is in this background that the approach paper to the Eleventh Plan (2007-12) has come out with a blue print for 'faster and inclusive growth'. It would, therefore, be appropriate to introspect the various odd facets of execlusionary growth in India and reflect the challenges of inclusion, not merely from the view point of growth per se but development in transformational sense so as to pave the way for a latent potential of including the excluded.

I. DEFINING INCLUSIVE DEVELOPMENT

The dictionary meaning of inclusion is to include the excluded. In this sense, the natural way of defining inclusive development is by opposition to the pattern of perverse growth, known as 'excluding' (from the consumer market) and 'concentrating' (of income and wealth) growth. Two additional features of excluding growth are:

- Strongly segmented labour markets which keep a large segment of toiling majority confined to informal activities, or else, condemned to eke out precarious livelihoods from small scale family farming with hardly any access to social protection.
- Feeble participation in political life, or outright exclusion from it, of large sections of population, poorly educated, under-organised and absorbed by daily struggle for mere survival, the women, subjected to gender discrimination, are the most hardly hit.

Inclusive development calls, first of all, at ensuring the exercise of civil, civic and political rights. Democracy is a truely foundational value (Sen, 1999), as it also guarantees the transparency and accountability necessary for the working of development processes. All the citizens must have access on equal basis to welfare programmes for disabled, mothers and children, and old age, directed at the compensation of natural or physical inequalities. The whole population should also have equitable opportunities of access of public services such as education, health protection and housing.

Market-led economy is commanded for its unparalleled efficiency in producing goods (wealth), but it also excels in producing social bads and environmental bads. For the ideologues of market fundamentalism these bads are the unavoidable price to be paid for economic progress. This argument rests, between, on a very narrow definition of efficiency. In an important book on the limits of the market Kuttner (1997), distinguishes three kinds of efficiency; the allocative one associated to the name of Adam Smith, the innovative one, (Schumpeterian), and the Keynesian one consisting of full employment of all the means of production. I argue two additional efficiencies are also essential: the social one (overlapping with the Keynesian as far as the full employment of manpower is concerned) and the eco-efficiency. Undoubtedly, market-led economic is quite efficient in allocative terms but deficient with respect to Keynesian social and eco-efficiencies, which are essential to the concept of inclusive, sustainable and sustained development, with decent work for all as its centre piece.

II. DECREASING INCLUSION IN INDIA: SALIENT FEATURES

There is no denying the fact that the process of socio-economic transformation leading to overall development has already started in the country. At the same time, there should not be any denial of the fact that the process has been too slow and there is a disturbing deceleration in the process of development accompanied by heightened disparities on a whole range of indications that signal the features of decreasing inclusion in India (See Table 1). The most visible one, including those explicitly recognised by the Approach Paper, are:

(i) A slowdown in the decline of absolute poverty as determined by the official poverty line despite a historically unprecedented high rate of growth of the economy.

(ii) A heightened disparity in income between agriculture and non-agriculture, rural and urban areas and above all the organised and unorganised sectors;

(iii) The persistence of much higher levels of poverty and deprivation among the socially weaker sections, especially those classified under SCs and STs;

(iv) The near stagnation in growth in employment in the organised sector despite an alarming decline in the share of wages and a corresponding increase in gross profits.

(v) The increasing divergence of states in overall growth and development;

(vi) The persistence of the divide between men and women in the quality of employment, earnings, opportunities and human developments indicators; and

(vii) The decline in the outreach of formal institutional support systems to the small producers (both agriculture and non-agriculture) in such areas as credit, extension and other development interventions.

Deposit the recognition of many of the these disturbing developments that pose a greater challenge for inclusion that before, the running themes of the Approach Paper are centred on the need for a higher rate of growth of 9 per cent per annum.

III. POVERTY INCIDENCE AND SOCIAL EXCLUSION UNDER REGIONAL DIMENSION

The contention that the first claim on inclusion belongs to those who are poor and deprived in the absolute sense can hardly be disputed. The record so far has been rather dismal and the period of economic reform has been less inclusive than before. It needs repetition that those who are poor and deprived are not people who do not contribute to the process of economic growth; on the contrary almost all of them are in the category of what may be called the 'working poor'. Almost every aspect of the problem of poverty and deprivation has a sharp regional dimension. And this includes such systemic problems as social exclusion, gender bias and the condition of children. It can, therefore, be argued that the focus has to be on the problem states (as proxy for

TABLE I

Increasing Growth and Decreasing Inclusion

Selected Indicators	*Pre-Refrom Period 1983-84 to 93-94*	*Post-Reform Period 1993-94 to 04-05*
1. Growth rate of the economy	5.18	6.30
2. Rate of decline in poverty	(-) 0.81	(-) 0.74
3. Rate of growth in real rural wages in agriculture (casual workers)	3.41	1.98
4. Rate of growth in real rural wages in non-agriculture (casual workers)	3.99	3.23
5. Share of wages in organised manufacturing	27	13
	1993-93	*1999-2000*
6. Sectoral product in agriculture as a percentage of non-agriculture	24	20
7. Sectoral product in rural economy as a percentage of the urban economy	34	30
	1999-2000	*2004-05*
8. Rates of unorganised to organised sector sectoral product	6.6	7.1
	1993-94	*2004-05*
9. Ratio of SC and ST poverty to Poverty of other population	2.28	2.51
	1993-94 over 83	*2004-05 over 94*
10. Growth rate of employment in all sectors	2.1	1.9
	1993-2000	*1999-2005*
11. Inter-state disparities in per capita income through coefficient of variations	36.6	128.2
	1993-94	*2004-05*
12. Ratio of female agricultural wage rate to male agricultural wage rate	0.70	0.69
13. Wage employment days for rural agricultural male labourers	244	227
14. Wage employment days for rural agricultural female labourers	196	184
15. Percentage of regular workers in total workers (UPSS)		
Urban Male	42.0	40.6
Urban Female	28.4	35.6
Rural Male	8.5	9.0
Rural Female	2.7	3.7

16.	Total institutional credit percentage distribution to sub-marginal farmers (less than 0.4 hectare)	-	2003 42.2
17.	Total institutional credit percentage distributions to medium large farmers (above 2 hect.)	-	66.8
18.	Total non-institutional % credit distribution to sub-marginal farmers	-	57.6
19.	Total non-institutional % credit distribution to medium large farmers	-	33.2

Note: The break point for post-reform period is based on the availability of statistics on employment, wages, etc. Although comprehensive policy changes were initiated during 1991-92, it is reasonable to assume that this impact was felt only after a lag of one or two years.

Source: Compiled and calculated from various sources such as Government of India, Economic Survey, various issues, Annual Survey of Industries, CSO, National Accounts Statistics, NSS, various rounds, etc.

regions) as the operational domain for concerted state interventions and mobilisation of other forms of public action. In order to bring this issue into sharp focus, we have selected a few basic indicators of income, poverty and deprivation, and classified the states as Under-performing States (UPS) and Better Performing States (BPS) corresponding to performance below the national average and above the national average, respectively. By this classification, more than half the states in India are BPS and their averages in many respects are indeed impressive as compared to their income levels. These are summarised in Table 2.

The problem of social exclusion is much stronger manifestation of inequality due to deeper barriers. Here one also finds a regional dimension. The incidence of poverty is being analysed first. The incidence of poverty among the SC and ST population is the highest in six states (see Table 3) with Maharashtra, one of the top prosperous states by per capita income, being at the top followed by not only the usual suspects of Orissa, Bihar, MP and UP, but also Tamil Nadu. However, from a social exclusion point of view (i.e. SC/ST poverty as a percentage of poverty of the other population), the picture is quite eye-opening. Punjab tops the list, which means that poverty in Punjab is now almost exclusively a problem facing the SCs (since there is hardly

TABLE 2

Regional Divide in Economic and Social Indicators in India

Indicator	*UPS* average	*BPS* average	*National* average
Growth rate in GSDP (1993-94 to 2004-05)	3.76[14]	6.73[14]	5.74[28]
Poverty			
Incidence of poverty (2004-05)	35.92[8]	19.0[20]	27.81[28]
Incidence of rural poverty (2004-05)	36.40[8]	18.41[20]	28.70[28]
Education			
Adult Literacy Rate (2001)	57[11]	73[17]	65[28]
School Dropout Rate (Class I to 10) (2002)	74[14]	46[11]	63[25]
Gross Enrolment Ratio (2002)	76[13]	100[15]	108[28]
Health			
Life Expectancy at birth (1998-02)	59.3[6]	65.4[9]	62.5[16]
MR (Boys) (2001)	66[8]	39[20]	56[28]
IMR (Girls) (2001)	72[8]	44[20]	61[28]
Women's Condition			
Mean age at marriage (1998-99)	19[5]	21[19]	20[24]
Women in anaemia (1998-99)	61[10]	46[14]	52[24]
Percentage of birth all by health profile (1998-99)	27[11]	63[12]	42[23]
Maternal mortality rate (1998-99)	588[5]	169[10]	407[15]
Total fertility rate (1998-99)	3.7[9]	2.3[15]	2.9[24]
Gender bias			
Female literacy as a percentage of that for males (2001)	61[10]	78[18]	71[28]
IMR of girls as a percentage of that for boys (2001)	109 [8]	144 [20]	109 [28]
Girls' dropout rate (Class I to 10) as a percentage of that for boys (2002)	119[8]	100[7]	107[25]
Social exclusion			
SC and ST literacy as a percentage of that of the other population (2001)	64[7]	78[14]	74[21]
SC and ST population (17 years and above) who completed at least Matriculation as a percentage of that of the other population excluding Muslims (2001)	40[5]	62[6]	50 [11]

Gender and social exclusion			
Rural female literacy rate of SCs and STs as a percentage of that for rural male SCs and STs (2001)	46[6]	66[15]	59[21]
Rural female literacy of SCs and STs as a percentage of that for all rural females (2001)	71[8]	85[13]	78[21]
Rural SC/ST females who have completed middle school as a percentage of all rural females (2001)	40[5]	75[6]	60[11]
Rural SC/ST females who have completed matriculation as a percentage of all rural females (2001)	28[4]	57[7]	43[11]

Note: Figures in square brackets indicate the number of states. The averages are weighted averages. For the growth rate of the economy, the weights refer to income and for all others, population weights have been used. UPS = Under-performing States (i.e. below the national average); BPS – Better Performing States (i.e. above the national average); (a) means including Chhattisgarh and Jharkhand; (b) means including Chhattisgarh,. Jharkhand and Uttaranchal; (c) means including Uttaranchal; (d) means including Chhattisgarh and Uttaranchal; (e) means including Jharkhand; (f) means including Jharkhand and Uttaranchal.

Source: Government of India, Economic Survey, various issues. Central Statistical Organisation (2004), National Family and Health Survey Report (1998-99), Census 2001, Government of Indian (2001), and Planning Commission (2002).

any ST community in the state). The situation is similar in Haryana as well. The picture emerging from a social exclusion point of view (see Table 4) is that it is a general problem, given the fact that the incidence of poverty among SCs/STs is two-and-a-half times higher than for the other population. But extreme forms of exclusion are found in seven states that have less overall poverty and high per capita income, and include states that are often praised and paraded for their pro-reform—often proactive—policies.

There are many dimensions of gender bias and equity in the economic sphere. However, the worst sufferers are women from the poorer households, in rural areas and those belonging to the socially weaker sections. There could be other layers on this bottom layer. First, there is the issue of narrow range of economic opportunities. Among the women workers in the country, 96 per cent are unorganised workers

TABLE 3

Higher Poverty among SCs/STs as Social Exclusion

State	*SC/ST poverty ratio*	*Poverty ratio of other population*	*SC/ST poverty as % of other population poverty*
Punjab	16.8	1.9	884
Haryana	24.9	4.8	519
Gujarat	36.6	7.8	469
Maharashtra	66.7	15.6	428
Tamil Nadu	53.6	12.9	416
Rajasthan	31.0	8.6	360
Andhra Pradesh	34.8	10.1	345
Orissa	77.2	28.1	275
India	47.9	19.1	251
Karnataka	36.6	15.2	241
Madhya Pradesh	58.8	24.6	239
Bihar	72.8	34.1	213
Kerala	24.1	11.3	213
Uttar Pradesh	51.3	25.7	200
West Bengal	38.5	22.4	172

Note: Incidence of poverty refers to the year 1999-2000.

as against the corresponding percentage of 89 for men. The percentage of women not able to secure minimum wages, as indicated before, is also quite high. Added to this is the trend in feminisation of agriculture and a few selected occupations because of the migration of men workers in search of better gainful opportunities.

But the biggest message is that national averages no longer convey any operational meaning as far as a large number of indicators of poverty and other forms of human deprivation are concerned. About one-third to one-half of the states need special attention. However, the core problem states whose under-performance contributes disproportionately to the poor national average are just seven in number or one-third of the total. They, however, account for close to half the population (45 per cent). These states are Madhya Pradesh, Orissa, Bihar, Uttar Pradesh, Rajasthan, Jharkhand and

TABLE 4

Poverty Incidence and Social Exclusion

Exclusionary	*High exclusionary*	*Extremely exclusionary*
(SC/ST poverty between 110 and 200% of total population poverty)	(SC/ST poverty between 201 and 300% of total population poverty)	(SC/ST poverty > 300% of total population poverty)
Total population poverty above 150% of the national average	Orissa [8, 275] Bihar [11, 213]	
Total population poverty above the national average but less than 150%	Uttar Pradesh [12, 200] West Bengal [13, 172]	Madhya Pradesh [10, 239]
Total population poverty between 50 and 150% of the national average	Karnataka [9, 241] India [251]	Gujarat [3, 469] Maharashtra [4, 428] Tamil Nadu [5, 416] Rajasthan [6, 360] Andhra Pradesh [7, 345]
Total population poverty less than 50% of the national average	Kerala [11,213]	Punjab [1, 884] Haryana [2, 519]

Source: Kannan (2007)

Chhattisgarh. Uttaranchal is a Better Performing State in many aspects pertaining to poverty and deprivation. A visual representation of these states shows that they form a contiguous geographical area from East to West with differential ecological characteristics. This points to the need for a serious examination of the social and economic institutions and forces that debilitate, here more than in the other states in the country, the process of economic development of a less exclusive nature.

Specific targets that can be monitored are, therefore, needed for the UPS since the BPS have already achieved a number of national targets. It is thus necessary for the Eleventh Plan (as well as for future Plans) to recognise that solutions based on 'one size that fits all' will no longer be effective. This calls for a national perspective and a framework within which individual states are not only enabled but also actively assisted to address region-specific problems and challenges.

IV. EMPLOYMENT: CRITICAL AGENDA FOR INCLUSION

Despite the overall objective of inclusive growth, the discussion on employment has been the core of the Eleventh Plan. Given the experience of the past 15 years, employment ought to be the central objective in the agenda of inclusive development and should be the common thread connecting the entire Plan exercise. The high growth performance during the Tenth Plan seems to have prompted the objective of achieving a growth rate of 9 per cent during the Eleventh Plan. However, there remains a major concern. How do we ensure that such a high rate of growth of the economy translates itself into productive employment.

We have estimated the employment implications of sectoral growth targets given in the Approach Paper. It is assumed that the GDP growth during the years 2005-06 and 2006-07 will be about 8 per cent with sectoral break-ups as revealed during the first three years of the Tenth Plan. It is further assumed that the labour force will grow at the same rate as current projections of the working age population indicated in the Approach Paper, which is about 2.3 per cent. The employment elasticities of each of the sectors, agriculture, industry and services, observed during the years 1993-94 to 2004-05 are also assumed to hold good during the period ranging from 2005-06 to 2011-12. On the basis of the above assumptions, it is estimated that the backlog of unemployed persons at the beginning of the Eleventh Plan will be about 35.2 million, which matches with the estimates given in the Approach Paper. However, the addition of labour force during the Plan period will be 58.1 million instead of 52 million (or 65 million) as projected in the Approach Paper. The number of persons for whom employment has to be generated during the Plan period is, therefore, 93.3 million (58.1+35.2). As against this target, the estimated employment generation will be about 69.1 million leaving a gap of about 24.2 million. The details of the calculation are given in Table 5.

TABLE 5

Employment Projections

Sector	*Employment in 2004-05 (Million)*	*Employment elasticity (1993-94 to 2004-05) (Percent)*	*Expected GDP growth 2005-07 (Million)*	*Projected employment (2006-07) (Percent)*	*Projected GDP growth 11th Plan (Million)*	*Projected employment 2011-12*
Assuming 9 per cent growth in GDP						
Agriculture	222.5	0.11	2.3	223.6	4.1	228.7
Industry	83.1	0.59	8.7	91.8	10.5	124.0
Services	121.1	0.44	9.8	131.7	9.9	163.7
Employed total	426.7		8.0	447.2	9.0	516.4
Labour force	461.0			482.5		540.6
Unemployed	34.3			35.2		24.2
Unemployment (%)	7.4			7.3		4.5
Assuming 8 per cent growth in GDP						
Unemployed						33.8
Unemployment (%)						6.3

Note: The employment growth rates have been worked on the basis of person days worked in a week. The estimated person days in 2004-05 were converted into persons by dividing with 6.28, which is the average number of days worked in a week.

Source: Kannan (2007).

In our view, the policy of reducing employment in agriculture by ten million during the Plan period as enunciated in the Approach Paper is not supported by any sound economic argument or acceptable logic. Given the employment elasticities observed during the period 1993-2004 to 2004-05 in the industry and services sectors, and the GDP growth targets, the employment in these sectors cannot achieve an annual growth rate of more than 5.16 per cent.

Thus, it will be difficult to realise an employment growth rate of 6 per cent as envisaged in the Approach Paper. Even if such a rate is achieved, it is likely to be by expanding self-employment in a manner that would be nothing but disguised unemployment.

Transferring labour from agriculture to the non-agriculture sector is desirable and is the classical route to structural transformation of the economy. What is not recognised in the Approach Paper is that such a transformation is already taking place in some of the states and it is not a countrywide problem but is concentrated in about 13 states in the country, in general, and seven states, in particular. By 2004, five states (Kerala, Tripura, Tamil Nadu, West Bengal and Punjab) had already achieved structural transformation in the sense of agriculture accounting for less than half of employment and income. Another ten have a share of employment between 50 and 60 per cent and at least half of them can be considered as candidates likely to achieve structural transformation by the end of the Eleventh Plan. On the bottom scale, there are at least seven states with an employment share in agriculture of more than 65 per cent. The rest have a share ranging between 61 and 65 per cent. The concentration of workers in agriculture is thus essentially a problem confined to 13 states out of 28 major states accounting for 29 per cent of the workers (Table 6). This means that the rate of growth of non-agriculture has to be much higher than the projected 6 per cent for these states which is unlikely to be achieved.

IV. CRISIS IN AGRICULTURE: CHALLENGE FOR SECTORAL EXCLUSION

Agriculture sector in India is currently passing through a crisis. The annual growth of agricultural output decelerated from 3.08 per cent pa during the period 1980-81 to 1991-92 to 2.38 per cent pa during 1992-93 to 2003-04 and the growth rate of crop output decelerated from 3.19 per cent p.a. during the 1980s to 1.18 per cent p.a. during the latter period. Similarly, the annual growth of food grains output decreased to an all time low of 1.16 per cent p.a. This annual growth is

during the Eleventh Plan. However, the approach paper is not explicit enough in its strategy to bring about an inclusive growth in agriculture.

VI. THE UNORGANISED SECTOR: LEADING EXCLUSIONARY SECTOR

The unorganised sector is one of the leading exclusionary sector of Indian economy, particularly on the ground of its vulnerability and decent work deficit. Despite significant strides made by the Indian economy over the past 60 years of political independence, an overwhelming proportion of the population (836 million or 77 per cent of the population) were living below Rs. 20 per day based on consumption expenditure. 79 per cent of the unorganised sector workers are in this category and are thus poor and vulnerable (NCEUS, 2007). Similarly providing decent employment is the challenge for all nations in the world, including India. It ranks high among the Millennium Goal. As we know that decent work/employment could be increased by increasing employment in organised sector. Unfortunately, the Annual Economic Survey (2007) confirms that the annual growth of employment in the organised sector has declined from 1.2 during 1983-94 to 0.38 during 1994-2004. It means that the organised sector has failed to generate additional employment, the burden of accommodating the entrants into the labour force has fallen on the unorganised sector. The quality of employment in the unorganised sector is, by definition, inferior to that of the organised sector particularly in terms of job security and social security perspective. However, it is not axiomatic that the quality of employment is better by being in the organised sector. The National Commission for Enterprises in the Unorganised Sector (NCEUS) has estimated that in 2004-05 almost one half (49 per cent) of the workers in the organised sector were unorganised/informal workers, who were not provided any job or social security by the employer. The corresponding figure was 46 per cent in 1999-2000. It evinces the fact that whatever the jobs created under organised sector have been informal.[1]

As on the January 2005, the total employment in the Indian economy was 458 million, of which the unorganised sector accounted for 395 million, that is, 86 percent of the total workers. Within the informal sector, 35 percent of the employment was in industry and services. The unorganised sector[1], including agriculture, contributes close to 60 percent of the national income. If the share of unorganised workers[2] in the organised sector were added, this would easily go up to 70 per cent.

From the date given in table 7, it is evident that out of the 62.6 million employed in the organised sector, 29.1 million are unorganised workers applying the criteria of social security benefits. Similarly out of 395 million workers employed in the unorganised sector, 1.4 million workers avail the benefits of social security and are therefore, classified as organised workers. After applying the two criteria out of a total employment of 457.5 million workers, only 34.9 million are entitled for social security benefits, that is, 7.6 per cent of total workers in 2004-05 and the remaining 422.6 million (92.4

TABLE 7

Sector-wise Total Employment (In Million)

Sector/Year	*Informal/Unorganised Workers*	*Formal/Organised Workers*	*Total*
1999-2000			
Informal/Unorganised Sector	341.3(99.6)	1.4 (0.4)	342.7(100.0)
Formal/Organised Sector	20.5(37.5)	33.6(62.2)	54.1(100.0)
Total	361.8(91.2)	35.0(8.8)	396.8(100.0)
2004-05			
Informal/Unorganised Sector	393.5(99.6)	1.4 (0.4)	394.9(100.0)
Formal/Organised Sector	29.1(46.6)	33.5(53.4)	62.6(100.0)
Total	422.6(92.4)	34.9(7.6)	457.5(100.0)

Note: Figures in brackets are percentages.

Source: NSS 61st Round (2004-05) and NSS 55th Round (1999-00), Employment, Unemployment Survey by NCEUS.

per cent) are treated as unorganised workers. Comparing this, with 1999-00, it is revealed that though during 1999-2000 and 2004-05, total employment in the economy incresed from 397 million to 458 million, that is an increase by 61 million during the five year period, the member of organised workers remained stagnant at 35 million and the entire increase of employment was in the category of unorganised workers. This contributes what can be termed as informalisation of the formal sector.

The greatest challenge, therefore, is to transform the unorganised sector of the economy into efficient units of production for ensuring a fair return to labour. Given the very small-scale nature of'the units, in both the agriculture and non-agriculture sectors, a changeover to the organised sector in the definitional sense (and by implication legal/ formal) as stated in the Approach Paper, is going to be a very long process. But strengthening them to make them efficient units of production would reduce the gap between the organised and unorganised sectors. This transformative agenda will be the core of the challenge of inclusive development in India in the years to come.

In fact, the Third Census of Small Scale Industries (2003) conducted by the Ministry of Small Scale Industries showed that 96 per cent of the enterprises belonged to the category of unorganised enterprises as per the NCEUS definition (i.e. private unincorporated with less than ten workers); the employment share was 83 per cent. But only 13 per cent of all enterprises were registered and the remaining were not registered and hence out of the purview of any benefits provided by the government.

The informal sector survey conducted by the National Sample Survey Organisation as a part of the NSS 55th Round, sought information on the problems faced by the enterprises. As per this survey, about 42 per cent of the enterprises reported shortage of capital as a major problem. It was uniformly high in both the rural and urban areas. The other major problems reported were local problems (19%), competition from larger units (17%) and lack of marketing and other infrastructure facilities (17%). Local problems and the problems of lack of marketing and other infrastructural facilities were more pronounced in rural areas. However, competition from larger units was experienced more by the urban enterprises.

The idea of Growth Poles is one such measure suggested by the NCEUS that has found a place in the Approach Paper for improving the condition of unorganised and other small-scale enterprises. The main content of this idea is the identification of existing clusters of enterprises in a given area to bring them under a proposed growth pole to provide and/or strengthen physical infrastructure such as roads, power, water, telecom as well as social infrastructure including institutions for training and skill formation/ upgradation and entrepreneurship, banking and financial institutions, information and marketing centres, healthcare and so on. Apart from strengthening public facilities such as transport, power and telecom connectivity, it also envisages the creation of common facilities including the purchase of inputs, warehouses, quality testing centres, packaging units, pollution/waste treatment facilities, drinking water, and so on. Such Growth Poles could also identify linkages with the concept of PURA (Provision of Urban services in Rural Areas—an idea propounded by ex-President Abdul Kalam)—and create enhanced economic integration between the Growth Poles and adjacent rural areas of economic growth potential.

RESUME

On the basis of the dismissions of the above six parts, the following conclusions are of major significance for the prospects of inclusive development in India. These are outlined below.

(i) The first claim on inclusion belongs to those who are poor and deprived in the absolute sense. These poor and deprived are not people who do not contribute to the process of economic growth; on the contrary almost all of them are in the category of what may be called the 'working poor'. Therefore, the challenge of overcoming poverty and deprivation has a work dimension. At the same time, the problem of poverty and deprivation has a sharp regional dimension. And this includes such systematic problems as social exclusion, gender bias and the condition of children. It can, therefore, be argued that the focus has to be on the problem states, classified as U.P.S. (i.e. socio-eco-indicators performances below the national average). Specific targets that can be monitored are, therefore, needed for the UPS. It is thus necessary for the XIth Plan to recognise the solution based on 'one size that fits all' will no longer be effective. Rather, state centric/region centric operational domain for concerted state intervention with target-oriented better mobilisation of delivery system is needed.

(ii) The second critical agenda for inclusion would be non-agricultural employment generation at over 6 per cent per annum during Eleventh plan and transforming labour from agriculture to non-agriculture sector. But, the given employment elasticites observed during the period 1993-2005 in the industry and services, the employment in these sectors cannot achieve an annual growth rate of more than 5.16 percent. Thus, it will be difficult to realise an employment growth rate of 6 percent as envisaged in the approach paper. Even if such a rate is achieved, it is likely to be by expanding self-employment in a manner that would be nothing but disguished unemployment.

As regards, the transforming labour from agriculture to non-agriculture sector, it is desirable but what is not recognised in the Approach Paper is that such a transformation is already taken place in some of the states and it is not a countrywide problem but is concentrated in about 13 states in the country, in general and seven states, in particular, accounting for 29 per cent of the workers. This means that the rate of growth of non-agriculture has to be much higher than the projected 6 per cent for these states which is unlikely to be achieved.

(iii) The third challenge for inclusion is concerned with the agriculture sector where sharp deceleration in agricultural growth and consequently stagnation in agricultural employment (0.9 percent p.a.) in noticed during reform period. The task then is, therefore, to convert the growth rate of agricultural sector to around 4 per cent (a tall order indeed) by doubling the public investment in agriculture and through adoption of two prolonged strategy, viz. (a) increasing demand for agricultural output on the one hand, and (b) increasing supply, on the other. However, the Approach Paper is not explicit in its strategy to bring about an inclusive growth in agriculture because special focus on dryland agriculture (59% of the total cropped area) has not been given in the Approach Paper.

(iv) Last but not the least, the challenge for inclusion is also concerned with unorganised sector and unorganised workers. It is because, the share of unorganised sector in national income has been estimated at being close to 60 per cent and unorganised workers accounted for 93 per cent of the total employment in the economy. But, 79 per cent of unorganised workers are living below Rs. 20 per day and thus are poor and vulnerable. Needless to mention that all unorganised workers are deficient in social security benefits.

What is, therefore, needed is directed intervention in the form of promotion for making this sector an efficient unit of production as well as essential protection of the unorganised workers within a transformational framework of development policy. The idea of Growth Pole is one such measure suggesed by NCEUS for improving the condition of unorganised sector and their workers as well as small scale enterprises. The main content of this idea is the identification of existing clusters of enterprises in given and to bring them under a proposed growth pole to provide and strengthen physical, social, financial infrastructures, information, marketing centres health centre and so on. Such Growth Poles could also identify linkages with PURA for pushing the concept of Growth Pole into a strategy for inclusive growth.

NOTES AND REFERENCES

1. The unorganised sector referes to enterprises, which imply less than ten workers (NCEUS, 2007).
2. The unorganised workers refers to workers who are employed whether in the organised or unorganised sector but are not covered for social security benefits.

REFERENCES

Bhalla, G.S. (2007): Indian Agriculture since Independence, NBT, N. Delhi.

Central Statistical Organisation (2004), Statistical Abstract of India, Government of India, New Delhi.

——— (2006), Economic Census, 2005, Government of India, New Delhi.

Government of India (2001), Selected Educational Statistics, 1999-2000, New Delhi.

——— (2004), Final Results: Third Census of Small Scale Industries, Development Commissioner (SS1), Ministry of Small Scale Industries, New Delhi.

——— (2007), Economic Survey, 2006-07, Ministry of Finance, New Delhi.

Kannan, K.P. (2007), Interrogating Inclusive Growth: Some Reflection on Exclusionary Growth and Prospects for Inclusive Development in India, *IJLE*, Vol 50, No. 1, January-March, 2007.

National Commission for Enterprises in the Unorganised Sector (NCEUS) (2007), Report on Social Security for Unorganised Workers, Government of India, New Delhi.

Plannmg Commission (2002), National Human Development Report, Government of India, New Delhi.

——— (2006), Towards Faster and Inclusive Growth: Approach Paper to the Eleventh Plan, Government of India, New Delhi.

6

The Process of Economic Growth of India

MAHESH CHANDRA PRASAD

In the context of globalisation, our problems cannot be discussed independently, without referring to some broader challenges addressed by the world community today. The provision of food security, employment and education for all is likely to be a greater problem than ever before, in view of the expected rise in population by nearly 3 billion people or 50 per cent in the next 3 decades to come. We should reckon the disheartening facts that 25 per cent of the world population lives in poverty and one-fifth of the people share hardly 1.4 per cent of the world's income. Further, environment deteriorates causing growing damage to the basic support systems of soil, water, flora and fauna and the atmosphere. Besides, the problems of less employment and gender discrimination bring to focus a number of adverse consequences at the economic, political and social spheres.

We may recall the recent occurrences in our history, related to economic reforms, since the time we entered the GATT agreement. The rationale of the introduction of reforms cannot be doubted. Already we have commenced our second generation reforms. Even now economists raise the three fold question, whether growth has trickled down, inequality widened and poverty deepened. Mostly, the answer is in the affirmative and hence our concern.

This paper examines the process of economic growth and its impact on development.

I. INTRODUCTION

In India, there has been a tendency to always look to the government for leadership on policy, processes, implementation and, then, to blame it for all our problems. The origin of its tendency lies in the centrality of government in social and economic activity—for example, the public sector and the "commanding heights" of the economy or the micro-controls on capacity and production or the ownership, control and management of the infrastructure. Basically, these policy framework existed for over four decades.

With the emergence of a competitive private sector, through its own entrepreneurship and restructuring (within the framework of government policy deregulation), there is some change in this thought process. Thanks to the economic reform policy followed by the government since 1991, and the trust and space provided to the private sector, Indian entrepreneurship has shown, in recent years, the ability to compete globally, to move our to international markets, to be investors abroad and to be both competitive and confident.

The Indian economy is on a bull run and has recently achieved a landmark Gross Domestic Product (GDP) of US$ 1 trillion. After witnessing a lull in the initial years of the current decade, India staged a come back with a huge bang. Over the last 5 years, India's GDP more than doubled to US$ 1 trillion, at a CAGR of 16 per cent. A higher GDP growth rate combined with a lower population growth rate has led to an accelerated growth in per capita GDP.

The economy today is strong and vibrant owing to the progressive liberalisation of government policies, an increase in foreign direct investment, increased global competitiveness, investment in infrastructure and the growth in domestic as well as international demand for Indian goods and services.

India ranks fourth in terms of Purchasing Power Parity, after the USA, China and Japan. India is home to the youngest population in the world—where half its citizens are under the age of 25. This growing working population in India is providing firepower to the growth of our economy.

The Next Trillion Dollar (NTD) Era: 2007 to 2012

According to Motilal Oswal's 12th Wealth Creation Study, released in December 2007, in the next five years India's GDP will hit US$ 2 trillion (assuming the current Re/ US$ parity). The growth rate in the NTD era will be almost the same as that of the last 5 years. However, given the high base, the GDP added in the next 5 years will be more than that which was added in the last 30 years, and twice that of the last 5 years.

II. PROCESS OF ECONOMIC GROWTH

On the tenth anniversary of independence, the Indian economy was in the first year of the Second Five Year Plan, which emphasized important substitution and public enterprise, a strategy that, in hindsight, may have imposed heavy costs on the economy. On the twentieth, we were reeling under the effects of a severe and persistent drought, for which, fortunately, a solution was not far away. On the thirtieth, the country was just coming to terms with the fact that there was an alternative to the Congress Party, however fractious and unstable it might be. Independent India turned thirty in a delicate balance between the burdens of its economic policies and the promise of its democratic potential.

The fortieth anniversary came when we were in the early, but unmistakable, phase of economic liberalisation and globalisation. We discovered that little liberalisation and globalisation can be dangerous, a development which actually turned out to be hugely beneficial. It precipitated a fundamental restructuring of the Indian economy, which was undoubtedly responsible for the significant improvement in economic performance that we have seen since then. Its fiftieth birthday saw India standing firm against a global wave that crippled some of its more successful neighbours.

Sometimes, it appeared, too much globalisation could be as dangerous as too little. However, it is the last decade—to be more precise, its latter half—that has provided dramatic and irrefutable evidence that an open and competitive economic environment induces better and better performances from the country's resources, human and otherwise.

As it turns sixty, there are good reasons to believe that the trajectory of the last few years will persist. Large and under penetrated domestic markets provide an enduring growth opportunity for most businesses. Intensifying domestic and global competition ensure that only the most efficient will survive, to the benefit of both consumers and investors. And, our large population, which appeared to be an unbearable burden in a previous, sadder, economic environment, is now seen as a productive resource that simply cannot be replicated by most of our competitors. Increasing global integration has progressively insulated us from virtually all forms of external turbulence, to an extent where we are now lamenting the pressures of managing excessive foreign exchange inflows!

Growing perceptions about the relatively benign impact of the political system also reinforce this confidence. The recent sense of gridlock and suboptimal consensus-seeking notwithstanding, the ability of any ruling coalition to fundamentally change the course of economic policy and sreverse the growing significance of a competitive private sector is rather limited. Apart from becoming shock-proof, the economy appears to be progressively becoming politics proof.

All these and some other factors support the assessment that the economy is in for a sustained period of fast growth in a relatively benign macro economic environment. However, one should not lose sight of the several threats that loom.

First, our languor in facilitating private investment in most infrastructure sectors has led to a widening gap between demand and supply. Productivity gains, both in producing and consuming sectors are helping us string things along, but this is stop-gap and simply cannot persist. Second, we have far too many people available to do several kinds of jobs that aren't being created, or worse, have fallen by the wayside because of obsolescence. Providing relevant and marketable skills to these hundreds of millions is necessary for the benefits of rapid growth to be spread widely. Third, the overall quality of public services, reflecting the capacity and efficiency levels of government, has deteriorated to a point where a great divide has been created between those who depend on these services and those who can afford private alternatives.

The list is not complete, but the essential point is that sustainability is by no means guaranteed. Even as we continue to insulate ourselves against external shocks, by our inaction and delays on several critical policy fronts, we intensify the risks of domestic disruptions. In the past, we have shown incapacity to change while things are going well, while responding with alacrity and competence to crisis. That tendency may well come to our rescue if things pan out that way, but why let things go that far? At this level of economic performance, a crisis can be very, very costly.

Also, over the last several decades, we should have learnt a simple, but fundamental lesson. Neither the public sector nor the private sector can carry the load of sustaining rapid growth exclusively. There is a critical complementarity between the two in both accelerating and maintaining economic performance. On its sixtieth birthday, the country has seen .the pendulum swing from the extreme of public sector dominance to the extreme of private sector self-reliance. It is tune that it settled in the middle—its own sustainable equilibrium—with recognition and exploitation of the full range of complementarities between the two sectors.

III. INDIA IS FLYING

Real gross domestic product (GDP) at factor cost has grown 9.4 per cent annually in the last three years (2004-05 to 2006-07). A key question is whether this rate represents a business cycle effect or fundamental shift in the trend growth rate.

The accompanying chart helps explain the complexity of the issue. In the first three years of the 1990s, the GDP grew 4 per cent annually. In the following four years, the growth rate jumped to 7.1 per cent but only to fall back to 5.2 per cent in the succeeding five years. Underlying these fluctuations, the trend growth rate was approximately 6 per cent.

In the late 1980s, the long-run growth rate had shifted up to 6 per cent from its prior level of approximately 4.5 per cent. Growth rate in the last three years shows signs of yet another break in the trend rate but it may also represent a sharp upturn in the business cycle, in which case the growth rate may decline significantly in the coming years. It will be two or three years before we feel confident of a shift in the trend.

Nevertheless, one thing about which we can be confident is that the Indian economy has produced some spectacular successes in the last three years not seen before—successes that rival the performance of the Chinese economy. In turn, these successes have fundamentally altered the initial conditions with important longer-term implications. These successes also raise doubts growth impulses in the economy.

The first striking observation is that the last three years, the economy has grown a phenomenal 19 per cent per annum in current dollars. In 1990-91, the GDP in current dollars was $317 billion. During the last three years, the GDP has increased by $327 billion. To put the matter even more dramatically, given the US inflation rate of 3 per cent, the GDP in real dollars grew at the annual rate of 16 per cent in the last three years. If this momentum can be sustained—a virtual impossibility—the Indian GDP would rise from its current level of $800 billion to cross the current US GDP of $512.5 trillion in just 20 years!

One important reason why this growth represents something very real is the near spectacular expansion of India's trade during the last three years. In 1990-91, merchandise export stood at $18.1 billion in current dollars. In the last year, exports increased by more than that amount. Alternatively, 1990-91 exports took nine years to double. In contrast, the recent doubling has taken place in just three years: from $ 52.7 billion in 2002-03 to $102.7 billion in 2005-06.

Services exports tell much the same story: from a low

level, they were multiplied by a factor of 3.5 during 10 years between 1990-91 and 2000-01. But starting from a much higher level, they were multiplied by 3.7 in just five years between 2000-01 and 2005-06. The ratio of goods and services exports to GDP rose from 11.6 per cent in 1999-00 to 15.6 per cent in 2002-03 and to 20.5 per cent in 2005-06. The latter change is dramatic since it took place in the presence of the GDP growth of 19 per cent per annum in current dollars.

Thanks to the rapid expansion of foreign portfolio investment, the total foreign investment flow has risen from $6 billion in 2002-03 to $20 billion in 2005-06. Remittances from abroad have risen less dramatically. But they too have gone up from $17 billion in 2002-03 to $25 billion in 2005-06.

The story in telecommunications is now quite well known. In 1990-91, India had just five million telephone lines in total. Currently, telephone lines are expanding at the rate of more than five million per month. In urban areas, teledensity has reached 31 per cent—a level unthinkable even five years ago. Teledensity in the rural areas at 2 per cent remains low. But to put the matter in perspective, as recently as 1991, urban teledensity. The communication sector as a whole has been growing 24 per cent per year in real terms since 1999-00. Its share in the GDP has more than doubled from 1.6 per cent in 1999-00 to 3.5 per cent in 2004-05.

Automobile sector offers yet another example of dramatic expansion. The sales of passenger vehicles have risen from 707,000 in 2002-03 to 1.14 million in 2005-06. The total turnover of the automobile industry rose from $12.3 billion in 2002-03 to $19 billion in 2004-05. Likewise, construction sector has shown robust growth of 12 per cent per annum in the last three years.

At least three factors distinguish the current expansion from the one during 1993-97. First, trade expansion and therefore integration into the world economy in the current phase has been much more rapid and deeper. Second, the exchange rate in the current phase has been either stable or has appreciated. This has meant a very rapid growth in the GDP in dollar terms when converted at the market exchange rate. Finally, after three consecutive years of 7 per cent plus growth, the previous phase saw growth rate plummet to 4.8

per cent. The current phase has so far shown no sign of slowing down.

But the current phase also shares one major weakness with the previous phase: labour-intensive manufacturing has remained sluggish. The end to licensing and to the small-scale industries reservation in most labour-intensive products has still not produced a major success in this sector. The reasons for this sorry phenomenon are well known (labour market rigidities facing large-scale producers, infrastructure bottlenecks and bureaucratic red tape). Unfortunately, without rapid expansion of the unskilled labour-intensive industry, progress towards poverty reduction and transition to a modern economy will re main far slower than is feasible.

IV. CONCLUSION

The investment in agriculture needs to be stepped up especially in the lagging regions. The backward and forward linkages of agriculture in poorer regions need to be emphasised more. Investment in water harvesting, soil conservation, rural roads, warehouses, processing activities and promotion of high value crops should be emphasised. Since agricultural growth is found to be more disparate, steps to equalise it will certainly reduce the regional imbalances.

Service sector has been found to be the new driver of the growth process. Especially, the banking and insurance sector and infrastructure have contributed to acceleration of many states. There is a need to promote these sectors, on priority, in backward regions.

Improvement in basic infrastructural facilities like power, transport, telecommunication and irrigation in backward states is a precondition to improve the quality of life of people and to usher in sustainable development in them. Availability of assured power supply, developed transport system and modern telecommunication facilities are important factors to attract private investments into these states.

The governments of backward states are fiscally weak and lack resources. Liberalisation process and various reforms have further weakened their financial position. It is hoped that resource flows to the states via Finance Commission awards and Planning Commission dispensation will continue and are likely to remain positively discriminating in favour of backward states. In fact, according to Rao (2000), these transfers are found to be progressive in reducing regional disparities. However, direct public sector investment by the central government in the states are likely to dry up gradually due to severe budget constraint of the Centre. Under the above circumstances, an important factor that influences the speed of economic progress of a state is the quality of governance. A better administered state is more efficient in raising revenues and putting them to better use. They are the states, which will attract more private investment both from domestic and foreign sources. Such states are also in a position to prepare viable projects and successfully bid central assistance or external funding. Hence, governance needs to be given immediate attention, especially in the backward states.

References

Anstey, Vera (1946), *The Economic Development of India*, Longmans, Green and Co., London.

Dadibhavi, R.V. and Bagulkoti, S.T. (2006), Reforms and Regional Inequalities in India, *The Indian Economic Journal*, Vol. 54, No. 2, July-September.

Datt, Gaurav and Ravallion, Martin (1997), "Macro Ecnomic Crises and Poverty Monitoring: A Case Study for India", *Review of Development Economics*, Vol. 1, No. 2.

Dreze, J. and Sen, Amartya (1999), *Indian Economic Development and Social Opportunity*, Oxford University Press, New Delhi.

Elango, R. (2005), Marginalised Population in India: Towards a Pro-poor Growth Process, *The Indian Economic Journal*, Vol. 53, No. 1, April-June.

Gokarn, S. (2007), Sustainability at Sixty: No Reason for Doubt, *Business Standard*, Kolkata, August 15.

Panagariya, A. (2006), Is India Finally Flying? *The Economic Times*, Kolkata, September 21.

—— (2007), India—A Trillion and Opportunity, *The Economic Times*, Kolkata, December 19.

Ravallion, Martin (2000), "What is Needed for a Pro-poor Growth Process in India?", *Economic and Political Weekly*, March.

Singh, R.K. (2004), *Economic Reforms in India* (ed.), Abhijeet Publications, New Delhi.

—— *The Economic Times* (2006), Kolkata, September 21.

—— *The Financial Express* (2005), Kolkata, October 28.

Role of Agriculture in Attaining Inclusive Growth in India

MD. TARIQUE

The key components of the 'inclusive growth' strategy must include a sharp increase in investment in rural areas, rural infrastructure and agriculture; spurt in credit for farmers; increase in rural employment through a unique social safety net; and a sharp increase in public spending on education and health care. The vision for inclusive growth lies in empowering the poor and as majority of the population in Bihar lives in rural areas depending on agriculture for their livelihood, the importance of agriculture sector in attaining inclusive growth in Bihar can't be denied. Even though yields on many crops in Bihar is still considerably lower than other states, an effective strategy for acceleration of productivity growth in agriculture has to tailor the right mix of actions to promote agriculture in the overall rural economy with the specific potentials of regions. The sector is important not only because of its contribution to the state's income and number of livelihoods dependent on it, but also because of the tremendous potential with which nature has endowed this sector. The escalation of agriculture sector will definitely be a step forward in the direction of attaining inclusive growth in Bihar.

I. INTRODUCTION

After passing through different stages of growth, the Indian economy is now poised towards a different trajectory which should not only be a reflection of high rate of magnification in the economy but also a move towards 'inclusive growth'. The term, inclusive growth, is finding its way increasingly in the lexicon of government leaders, economists, planners, academicians and businessmen, not just in India but even internationally. Robert Zoellick, president of the World Bank group, focussed on the theme of 'An Inclusive and Sustainable Globalisation,' at a recent meet in Washington DC. "Globalisation must not leave the 'bottom billion behind," remarked the new chief of the World Bank. "This assertion is based on more than respect for the worth of our fellow men and women, and beyond an appreciation that any of us might have been born in similar circumstances. Inclusive globalisation is also a matter of self-interest. Poverty breeds instability, disease, and devastation of common resources and the environment. Poverty can lead to broken societies that can become breeding grounds of those bent on destruction and to migrations that risk lives."

According to our Prime Minister, Manmohan Singh, the key components of the 'inclusive growth' strategy must include a sharp increase in investment in rural areas, rural infrastructure and agriculture; spurt in credit for farmers; increase in rural employment through a unique social safety net; and a sharp increase in public spending on education and health care. Further, there must be some Government interventions through legislative measures to empower the socially disadvantaged section of the society.

On the eve of the 11th Plan, our economy is in a much stronger position than it was a few years ago. After slowing down to an average growth rate of about 5.5 per cent in the 9th Plan period (1997-98 to 2001-02), it has accelerated significantly in recent years. The average growth rate in the last four years of 10th Plan period (2003-04 to 2006-07) is likely to be a little over 8 per cent, making the growth rate 7.2 per cent for the entire 10th Plan period. Though, this is below the 10th Plan target of 8 per cent, it is the highest growth rate achieved in any plan period.

The 11th Plan endows with a prospect to streamline policies to accomplish a new imagination. It should be based on faster, more diverse and inclusive growth, designed to reduce poverty and bringing together the various breaks up that continue to fragment our society. The 11th Plan must aim at putting the economy on a sustainable growth trajectory with a growth rate of approximately 10 per cent by the end of the Plan period. It will create productive employment at a faster pace than before, and target robust agriculture growth at 4 per cent per year. It must seek to reduce disparities across regions and communities by ensuring access to basic physical infrastructure as well as health and education services to all. It must recognise gender as a cross-cutting theme across all sectors and commit to respect and promote the rights of the common person. The first steps in this direction were initiated in the middle of the 10th Plan based on the National Common Minimum Programme adopted by the government. These steps must be further strengthened and consolidated into a strategy for the 11th Plan.

A key element of the strategy for inclusive growth must be an all out effort to provide the mass of our people the access to basic facilities such as health, education, clean drinking water, etc. While in the short run these essential public services impact directly on welfare, in the longer run they determine economic opportunities for the future. It is important to recognise that access to these basic services is not necessarily assured simply by a rise in per capita income. Governments at different levels have to ensure the provision of these services and this must be an essential part of our strategy for inclusive growth. At the same time it is important to recognise that better health and education are the necessary pre-conditions for sustained long-term growth. All these are possible if the people in 'have not' category are shifted to 'have ones' category. It is in this backdrop that this paper tries to examine the issue of inclusive growth with special reference to Bihar. The entire paper is divided into four segments. The first part is introductory one defining the basic terminology of inclusive growth and its importance for our economy. The second part discusses the strengths of the Indian economy under whose shadows now we are trying to adopt the inclusive growth model. The third part argues about the issue of inclusiveness with special reference to Bihar and how development of agriculture sector could be an important component in accomplishing the inclusive growth in the state. The final part of the paper is given to the concluding observations.

II. STRENGTHS OF INDIAN ECONOMY

The strengths of our economy are reflected in the macroeconomic indicators in Table 1 which compare the position in the 10th Plan with that of the 9th Plan. Compared to the 9th Plan, the pace of growth of the economy has accelerated and our macroeconomic fundamentals are sound.

- Domestic savings rates have been rising and reached 29.1 per cent in 2004-05.
- The combined fiscal deficit of the Centre and state governments is higher than it should be, but has been falling and the Budget Estimates for 2006-07 suggest it may come down to 7 per cent.
- Inflation has been moderate despite the sharp hike in international oil prices.
- The current account was in surplus during the first two years of the 10th Plan but in deficit to the extent of 1.0 per cent of the GDP in the third year, i.e., 2004-05. The deficit is estimated to have risen to around 1.3 per cent of the GDP during 2005-06 reflecting the revival of investment and also the impact of high oil prices; but a deficit of this order is eminently financeable.
- As of August 25, 2006 our foreign exchange reserves are at a very comfortable level at $ 165.3 billion.

TABLE 1

Macroeconomic Indicators	*9th Plan (1997-98 to 2001-02)*	*10th Plan (2002-03 to 2006-07)*
GDP growth (%) of which	5.5	7.2
• Agriculture	2.0	1.7
• Industry	4.6	8.3
• Services	8.1	9.0
Gross Domestic Savings (% of GDP, at market prices)	23.1	28.2
Gross Domestic Investment (% of GDP, at market prices)	23.8	27.5
Current Account Balance (% of GDP, at market prices)	-0.7	0.7
Combined Fiscal Deficit of Centre and States (% of GDP at market prices)	8.8	8.4
Foreign Exchange Reserves (US $ billion)	54.2	165.3
Rate of Inflation (based on WPI)	4.9	4.8

Source: 11th Five Year Plan Document, Planning Commission, GOI, 2006.

In the light of the performance of the economy during 10th Plan, the targets for the 11th Plan were set on an optimistic note. These targets are shown in the Table 2. Rapid growth is an essential part of our strategy for two reasons. Firstly, it is only in a rapidly growing economy that we can expect to sufficiently raise the incomes of the mass of our population to bring about a general improvement in living conditions. Secondly, rapid growth is necessary to generate the resources needed to provide basic services to all. Work done within the Planning Commission and elsewhere suggests that the economy can accelerate from 8 per cent per year to an average of around 9 per cent over the 11th Plan period, provided appropriate policies are put in place. With population growing at 1.5 per cent per year, 9 per cent growth in GDP would double the real per capita income in 10 years. This must be combined with policies that will ensure that this per capita income growth is broad-based,

TABLE 2

Macroeconomic Indicators for the 11th Five Year Plan	*10th Plan (Actual)*	*11th Plan (Average)*
I. Growth rate of GDP (%) of which;	7.2	9.0
a. Agriculture	1.7	4.1
b. Industry	8.3	10.5
c. Services	9.0	9.9
II. Investment rate (% of GDP) of which;	27.8	35.1
a. Public	6.7	10.2
b. Private	21.1	24.9
III. Domestic Savings rate (% of GDP) of which;	28.2	32.3
a. Household	22.8	22.0
b. Corporate	4.5	6.1
c. PSEs	4.2	3.0
d. Government	-3.2	1.2
IV. Current account balance (% of GDP)	0.2	-2.8
V. Government revenue balance (% of GDP)	-4.4	-0.2
VI. Government fiscal balance (% of GDP)	-8.0	-6.0

Source: 11th Five Year Plan Document, Planning Commission, GOI, 2006.

benefiting all sections of the population, especially those who have thus far remained deprived. While India has been growing very rapidly—even with some acceleration in the last few years—international experience shows that a recipe for slow growth is complacency about pushing ahead with reforms when growth is high. Most countries with rapid growth in any one decade show marked deceleration of growth rates in the next. India has so far been able to avoid that, as adroit response to an incipient slow-down in the 1990s restarted another episode of rapid growth. The reform momentum has been sustained across changes in government so that the basic direction of reform continues.

III. REGIONAL GROWTH AND INCLUSIVENESS

The Government of India's justifiable concern with the inclusiveness of economic growth can be addressed by focusing on expanding the regional scope of economic growth, expanding access to assets and thriving markets and expanding equity in the opportunities for the next generation of Indian citizens no matter whom they are or where they live. While reforms that are growth accelerators are important, even more pressing is the need for equalising accelerators—actions that promote more rapid growth in those areas, sectors and groups where it is needed the most. As the growth of the nation depends upon the proper growth of individual states, this portion of the paper discusses the prospects of achievement of inclusive growth in Bihar and the importance of agriculture sector in this direction. However, the infrastructural development, health, education and empowerment of the socially deprived section of the society are also important from the point of view of achieving inclusive growth. Recently our Prime Minister has said that the vision for inclusive growth lies in empowering the poor and as majority of the population in Bihar lives in rural areas depending on agriculture for their livelihood, the importance of agriculture sector in attaining inclusive growth in Bihar can't be denied.

In spite of the efforts of planned development in the past several decades, the regional disparities have widened and several states like Bihar are at the lowest rung of the development indicators. Infrastructural developments like roads, power, health and sanitation and other socio-economic indicators are abnormally poor compared to developed States. The backwardness of Bihar is due to historical reasons—low per capita plan expenditure, inadequate central assistance, recurrence of floods and droughts, low C-D ratio, etc. The bifurcation of the State has added further miseries to it. With 46 per cent of land transferred to Jharkhand, it has to sustain 75 per cent of population of the undivided State, leading to an extremely high density of population. The land area transferred to Jharkhand was very rich in mineral wealth, power plants, industrial units and human development institutions. The bifurcation of the State has had its impact on income and revenue raising capacity of the State and consequent fall in State Domestic Product has been of the order of 40 per cent while revenue receipts have fallen by 33 per cent. As a result of bifurcation, the State has become deficient in natural resources and minerals including coal which has impeded its industrial development. For a long term solution of this problem of energy deficiency, the State should be assigned mining blocks and not mere coal linkages. The National Plan should look into this problem in order to bring Bihar on the targeted industrial growth path.

Bihar, even with the separation of Jharkhand, still remains the third most populous state of the country with a population of 83 million people. More than 41 per cent of the population lives at the below poverty line level which is next to Orissa. Further a large gap exists between rural and urban poverty which is 42.10 per cent and 34.60 per cent respectively (Planning Commission, 2004-05). The figure clearly reflects that poverty is a major hurdle in the growth of Bihar and if inclusive growth is to be achieved, it has to be tackled first. As majority of the population in Bihar lives in rural areas and with the existence of a large gap in rural and urban poverty, the poverty in this state remains a rural phenomenon. Hence there is a need to improve the conditions of rural population and as the rural population mainly depends on agriculture sector, a care for agricultural sector will take care of the menace of poverty.

Bihar's economy over the years has experienced little structural change and is not well diversified. It is a predominantly agrarian economy with a small manufacturing base. While the share of agriculture has declined, it remains very large, the share of industry has remained stagnant, and services sector has increased its share from 41 per cent to nearly 50 per cent of GSDP, which is in line with the national average. The growing contribution of services sector in GSDP is a good sign from the point of view of developmental aspect of the state but it is simultaneously increasing the rural-urban gap and the income disparity within the urban and rural areas. To reduce the income inequality proper thought must be given to the development of the agriculture sector, apart from infrastructural development which provides a base for the sustainable development for any economy.

The bifurcation of the state in 2000 had an impact on the structure of the economy; the state of Jharkhand was created from the industrially advanced and mineral-rich southern-half of the state. The contribution of the secondary sector, which was 15.39 per cent in 1980-81, rose to 20.98 per cent in 1990-91 and fell to 10.55 per cent in 2000-01, less than half the share of the secondary sector nation-wide which is around 25 per cent. Agriculture constitute the backbone of Bihar's economy still contributing around 35 per cent of the GSDP and employing more than 70 per cent of the workforce. The state has the ideal natural resources: fertile flat land, plenty of water, both surface and underground, and agroclimatic conditions suitable for cultivating a variety of crops to make agriculture its core competence. Bihar has a geographical area of 93.6 lakh hectares, which has been categorised into three agro-climatic zones, namely, North-West Alluvial Plane (Zone 1), North-East Alluvial Plane (Zone 2) and South Alluvial Plane (Zone 3), with Zone 3 having further sub-classification of Zone 3A and Zone 3B (Appendix I). As agricultural practice is sensitive to agro-climatic conditions, one also finds great variations across the zones in terms of land utilisation, cropping pattern and cropping intensity. While agriculture is found to be most extensive in the north-western part of the state, its expanse in the southern part, in particular in the south-east, is found to be substantively lower. Net sown area in Zone 1 is 65.43 per cent of its geographical area, while the net sown area in Zone 3A is only 42.20 per cent of its geographical spread. The corresponding figures for Zone 2 and Zone 3B being 63.81 per cent and 57.06 per cent respectively. Cropping intensity is found to be the highest in the North-Eastern part of the state, with 36 per cent of its geographical area being sown more than once with the corresponding figures for the southern part falling to 6.56 per cent and 8.66 per cent for Zone 3A and Zone 3B respectively (Table 3). Here, it is pertinent to note that it is the North-East Zone which receives the earliest and highest rainfall in the state. Bihar not only has one of the most fertile soils in the country, but is also endowed with abundant water resources. Geographical location and spread further endow the state with an agro-climatic diversity which is pregnant with possibility of a vibrant agricultural sector, led by high value added agro-processing sector based on a vast and stable agricultural base.

In Bihar, agriculture was not benefited from the Green

TABLE 3

Land Utilisation Pattern (in per cent) across the Agro-Climatic Zones in Bihar

Sl. No.		*Zone I*	*Zone II*	*Zone IIIA*	*Zone IIIB*
1.	Forests	2.66	0.17	15.16	11.84
2.	Barren and Unculturable land	2.94	5.57	9.56	4.13
3.	Land Put to Non-Agricultural Use	19.91	18.05	16.94	14.80
	(i) Land Area	15.32	13.48	12.95	12.30
	(ii) Water Permanent	2.58	3.27	1.64	1.38
	(iii) Water Temporary	2.01	1.30	2.36	1.12
4.	Culturable Waste Land	0.16	0.36	1.90	0.39
5.	Permanent Pasture and Grazing land	0.17	0.16	0.36	0.16
6.	Land Under Miscellaneous Tree Crops and Groves	4.25	3.38	1.41	0.52
7.	Fallow other than current Fallow	0.72	1.72	2.85	1.48
8.	Current Fallow	3.78	6.77	9.62	9.63
9.	Total Unculturable Land (3+4+5+6+7+8)	34.59	36.19	57.80	42.94
10.	Net Sown Area	65.43	63.81	42.20	57.06
11.	Area Sown More than Once	24.55	36.09	6.56	8.66

Source: Department of Agriculture, Government of Bihar.

Revolution that ushered in a significant increase in productivity in several states in the country. The growth of food grain production at less than 1 per cent over the last decade has been far below potential; food grain production has increased from an average of 106.38 lakh MT in the mid-1990s (1993-94 to 1995-96) to 113.23 lakh MT in recent years (2000-01 to 2003-04). Low crop productivity, poor connectivity between farms and markets, and weak distribution and marketing links have meant that much of the vast demand from Bihar's local market is met by produce from outside the state, such as fish from Andhra Pradesh and milk powder from Gujarat. Even the local feed producers buy their maize from Andhra Pradesh, while Bihar's maize producers have to resort to distress sales to get rid of their produce. Cereals dominate the cropping pattern. The rice-wheat cropping system occupies more than 70 per cent of the gross cropped area, but productivity has remained low despite very favourable soil, water and climatic conditions. Many reasons technological, managerial and situational are attributable to the low productivity of crops in the state.

In the backdrop of above mentioned observations a road map for development of agriculture has been prepared under guidance of ICAR/RAU scientists. With implementation of the road map, it is expected that there shall be a substantial boost to agricultural productivity and income level of farmers. Through the activities under this road map, by the year 2012, following milestones are projected to be achieved:

- Enhancement of Crop Productivity
    1. Rice 14.86 Qtls/ha to 29.72 Qtls/ha.
    2. Wheat 20.55 Qtls/ha to 30.50 Qtls/ha.
    3. Maize 26.71 Qtls/ha to 35.25 Qtls/ha.
    4. Pulses 7.22 Qtls/ha to 10.13 Qtls/ha.
    5. Oil seeds 10.32 Qtls/ha to 12.00 Qtls/ha.
    6. Sugarcane 455.6 Qtls/ha to 600.00 Qtls/ha.
    7. Fruits 109.32 Qtls/ha to 146.05 Qtls/ha.
    8. Vegetables 165.92 Qtls/ha to 200.60 Qtls/ha.
- Enhancement of Crop intensity from 133 per cent (2004-05) to 161 per cent.
- Per-capita annual agricultural production to increase from Rs. 661 (2004-05) to Rs. 1300.
- The land productivity level in value terms to increase from Rs. 7351 (2004-05) to Rs. 14000.

Note: Present productivity figures relate to 2006-07 for fruits and 2005-06 for vegetables, target figures relate to 2012.

For the first time in Bihar on 17th Feb. 2008 'Kisan Panchayat' was organised and attended by the Chief Minister himself. On the basis of the advice of the farmers the road map for the development of Bihar's agriculture was framed and it is proposed to spend Rs. 4707 crores on the development of agriculture sector by 2012. The government has further announced to celebrate the year 2008-09 as 'Agriculture Year'.

While the state is very richly endowed with water resources, their spatial and temporal distribution have been a source of perennial problem which are to be seen in simultaneity of floods and drought in different regions of the state. Interlinking of rivers is being planned as a step towards integrated water management which would generate additional irrigation capacity, alleviate problems of floods and droughts and also facilitate simultaneous development of indigenous irrigation system.

In order to achieve success in the agriculture sector, the state Finance Minister in his budget speech 2008-09 has categorically said that as 90 per cent of the population in Bihar are directly or indirectly dependent on the agriculture sector, we want an all-round development of this sector and this could be achieved through a 'rainbow revolution' in the sector which will include not only traditional crops but also the growth of livestock, poultry, fisheries, horticulture, floriculture, medicinal plants and vermin compost, etc. The achievements that we couldn't make under green revolution shouldn't be treated as drawback rather it should be considered as an opportunity that large potentials are hidden for the development of this sector in our economy. To achieve the purpose, the Government of Bihar is continuously increasing the allocation for the development of the agriculture sector. This is clear from Table 4 which shows the expenditure on agriculture during the last few years.

TABLE 4

Expenditure on Agriculture in Bihar

(Rs. Crores)

Year	*2004-05*	*2005-06*	*2006-07*	*2007-08*	*2008-09*
Expenditure	59.81	20.43	95.39	133.45	191.34

Source: Budget Speech, 2008-09.

IV. CONCLUDING OBSERVATIONS

One of the foremost apprehensions with the pattern of growth is the deceleration in agriculture and the effect that has on the rural economy and particularly on employment and wages (as rural and urban markets for casual labor are increasingly linked). Even though yields on many crops in Bihar is still considerably lower than other states, an effective strategy for acceleration of productivity growth in agriculture has to tailor the right mix of actions to promote four directions for agriculture in the overall rural economy with the specific potentials of regions:

- *Intensification*: increased cropping intensity of traditional crops via irrigation, HYVs, agro-chemicals, mechanisation (Green Revolution).
- *Diversification*: shift to new more profitable crops (fruits, vegetables, higher value cereals, medicinal plants) and livestock.
- *Non-farm linkages*: emphasis on value addition, trading, agro-processing, input supply.
- *Exit from agriculture*: recognising that as productivity increases fewer people will need to be employed in agriculture, and that the long-term strategy in areas with limited agricultural potential is off-farm activities.

To achieve the above mentioned goals, the Budget 2008-09 of the state government articulates to bring 'rainbow revolution' in the agriculture sector and the year 2008-09 has been announced to be treated as 'Agriculture Year' in Bihar. Though the growth rate of agriculture in Bihar during the 10th Five Year Plan was merely 0.96 per cent, the government has set a target of achieving 5.70 per cent growth in the sector during the 11th Five Year Plan and it is expected that poverty rate in the state will go down from 41.5 per cent in 2004-05 to 28.4 per cent during the 11th Five Year Plan period. The sector is important not only because of its contribution to the state's income and number of livelihoods dependent on it, but also because of the tremendous potential with which nature has endowed this sector. The escalation of agriculture sector will definitely be a step forward in the direction of attaining inclusive growth in Bihar.

References

Addressing the Annual General Meeting of the Confederation of Indian Industry (CII) in 2007.

The growth Rate for 2006-07 is as Projected by the Economic Advisory Council to the Prime Minister.

Gross Savings Rate, Gross Investment Rates, and the Current Account Balance are expressed in current prices and are averages for the Plan. For the 10th Plan, these are the average of the first three years, i.e., for the years 2002-03 to 2004-05.

Combined Fiscal deficit is the Average of the Plan. For the 10th Plan, it is the average of the first 4 years of the Plan, i.e., for the years 2002-03 to 2005-06.

Foreign Exchange Reserves are as on 29th March, 2002 for the 9th Plan and 31st March, 2006 for the 10th Plan.

The rate of inflation for the 10th Plan is the average up to January 2006.

GDP growth rate is actual up to 2005-06 and as estimated by the EAC to PM for 2006-07. Savings rate, investment rate and CAB are actual up to 2004-05.

Government fiscal balance and revenue balance are based on actuals (3 years for Centre and two years for States) and for remaining years RE/BE/Projected.

Planning Commission figures for 2004-05 based on Uniform Recall Period (URP) consumption in which the consumer expenditure data for all the items are collected from 30 day recall period.

Economic Survey of Bihar, Government of Bihar, Finance Deptt., 2007-08.

Strategy for Accelerated and Inclusive Growth for Indian Economy with Special Focus on Agriculture

Padmini Prasad

SITUATION ANALYSIS

Indian Economy Overview

India's economy is growing rapidly by historical and global standards. India's growth began to accelerate in the 1980s and continued after the reforms of the early 1990s, perhaps at a modestly faster pace. This acceleration has taken India from being a below-average growth performer in the 1960s and 1970s to one of the most rapidly growing economies in the world in the 1990s.

The economy has been growing at an average growth rate of 8.8 per cent in the last four fiscal years (2003-04 to 2006-07), with the 2006-07 growth rate of 9.6 per cent being the highest in the last 18 years. Significantly, the industrial and service sectors have been contributing a major part of this growth, suggesting the structural transformation underway in the Indian economy.

For example, industrial and services sectors have logged in a 10.63 and 11.18 per cent growth rate in 2006-07 respectively, against 8.02 per and 11.01 cent in 2005-06. Similarly, manufacturing grew by 8.98 per cent and 12 per cent in 2005-06 and 2006-07 and transport, storage and communication recorded a growth of 14.65 and per cent 16.64 per cent, respectively.

Another significant feature of the growth process has been the consistently increasing savings and investment rate. While the gross saving rate as a proportion of GDP has increased from 23.5 per cent in 2001-02 to 34.8 per cent in 2006-07, the investment rate-reflected as the gross capital formation as a proportion of GDP has increased from 22.8 per cent in 2001-02 to 35.9 per cent in 2006-07.

The Current Fiscal Year

The process continues in the current fiscal year. On the back of 9.9 per cent growth in the first half of 2006-07, GDP grew by 9.1 per cent during April-September 2007.

- While overall industrial production grew by 9 per cent during April-December 2007, importantly capital goods production rose by 20.2 per cent compared to 18.6 per cent during same period in 2006.
- Services grew by 10.5 per cent in April-September 2007, on the back of 11.6 per cent during the corresponding period in 2006-07.
- Manufacturing grew by 9.6 per cent during April-December 2007, on the back of 12.2 per cent growth during same period in 2006-07.
- Core infrastructure sector continued its growth rate recording 6 per cent growth in April-November 2007.
- While exports grew by 21.76 per cent during April-December 2007, imports increased by 25.97 per cent in the same period.
- Money Supply (M3) has grown by a robust 22.8

per cent growth (year-on-year) as of December 21, 2007 compared to 19.3 per cent last year.
- The annual inflation rate in terms of WPI was 3.5 per cent for the week ended December 29, 2007 as compared to 5.89 per cent a year ago.
- Fiscal and revenue deficit decreased by 11 per cent and 17.2 per cent, respectively, during April-November 2007-08 over corresponding period last year.

Per Capita Income

Along this significant acceleration in the growth rate of Indian economy, India's per capita income has increased at a rapid pace, exceeding an earlier forecast made by Goldman Sachs BRIC report which estimated India's per capita to touch US$ 800 by 2010 and US$ 1149 by 2015.

Per capita income has increased from US$ 460 in 2000-01 to almost double to US$ 797 by the end of 2006-07. In 2007-08, India's per capita income is estimated to be over US$ 825.07, according to the advance estimates of the Central Statistical Organisation (CSO). Further, India's per capita income is expected to increase to US$ 2000 by 2016-17 and US$ 4000 by 2025. This growth rate will, consequently, propel India into the middle-income category.

The Economic Survey (2007-08) Highlights:

- Sets a target of 9 per cent GDP growth during the 11th Plan (2007-2012).
- Projected that inflation would stand at 4.4 per cent during the current fiscal.
- Forecast a lower agriculture growth at 2.6 per cent in 2007-08 as against 3.8 per cent in 2006-07, and a slow down in manufacturing sector growth at 9.4 per cent in the current fiscal from 12 per cent in FY07.
- Rupee up 9.8 per cent *vs.* Dollar, since April 2007.
- Economy slows down to 8.7 per cent in 2007-08, compared to 9.6 per cent in previous fiscal.
- Manufacturing sector to grow at 9.4 per cent in current financial year, lower from 12 per cent in 2006-07.

- Government sets target of 9 per cent GDP growth during 11th Five Year Plan (2007-12).
- Outlook for exports in 2008-09 may not be as bright due to global slowdown and exchange rate development.
- Foreign reserves at US$ 290.8, up by US$ 91.6 billion from a year ago.
- Total food grains production marginally high at 219.3 million tons in 2007-08 from 217.3 million tons last year.
- The agriculture, forestry and fishing sector is estimated to grow at 2.6 per cent during 2007-08, as against the previous year's growth of 3.8 per cent.
- Talent shortage leading to high attrition and rising wages, contributing to cost-push inflation.
- The Economic Survey favours liberalising debt and currency markets; removal of constraints on agriculture and urban land supply.
- Export growth at 20.3 per cent in 2007.
- Number of telephone connections at 272.88 million as on December 31, 2007; tele-density at 23.9 per cent.
- The government has set an ambitious target of providing 200 million telephone connections in the rural areas by the end of 2012.
- The rate of growth of per capita income has sharply climbed to 7.2 per cent p.a.—implying that average income can virtually double in a decad.
- India April-Nov. 2007 FDI at US$ 11.14 billion; Raise FDI in insurance, retail.
- Food procurement, distribution spend up in FY 2007-08.
- Greater debt and equity issues in primary market.

Unfortunately, in the Budget the next day, the government did not quite firm up its mind on most of the pre-requisites for a 9 per cent and higher growth rate.

Current Scenario (March 2008)

"The slowdown in the US economy could affect the growth rate of India. India achieved eight per cent plus growth rate over the last three years, when the global economy was doing well,"—Kemal Dervis, Administrator of UNDP, Tuesday, 18 March, 2008.

"The world economy has slowed down, every economy has slowed down. India is not an exception," Ahluwalia.

The 2008/09 growth forecast by Ahluwalia, one of the top economic advisers to Prime Minister Manmohan Singh, is below Finance Minister P. Chidambaram's estimate of at least 8.8 percent. Yaga Venugopal Reddy, India's central bank governor, said in January that India should aim for growth of at least 8.5 percent in the fiscal year 2008/09.

India needs faster industrial production to lift economic growth, which is expected to be 8.7 percent in the year to March 31, the slowest in the last three years. Still, growth will have averaged 9.2 percent since 2005, the quickest pace since India's independence in 1947 and behind only China among the world's major economies.

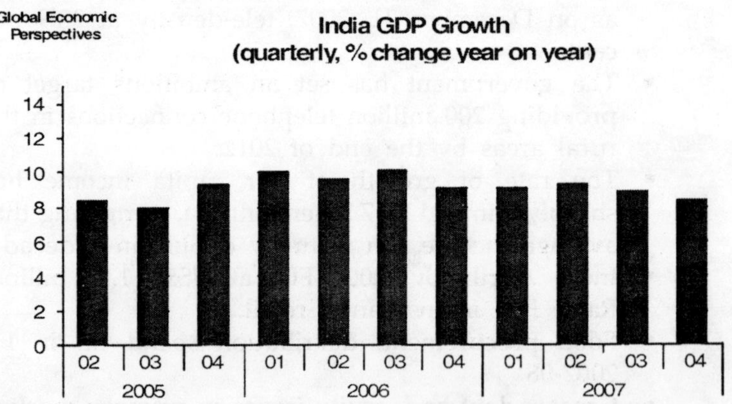

Industrial Output

Industrial output growth in January registered a 10-month low of 5.3 per cent against 11.6 per cent in the same. he fall took place chiefly because of an unexpected decline in capital goods and a continuing downtrend in consumer durables month last year and a revised 7.7 per cent in December, raising doubts over whether India will grow at 9 per cent in fiscal 2007-08.

The fall took place chiefly because of an unexpected decline in capital goods and a continuing downtrend in consumer durables.

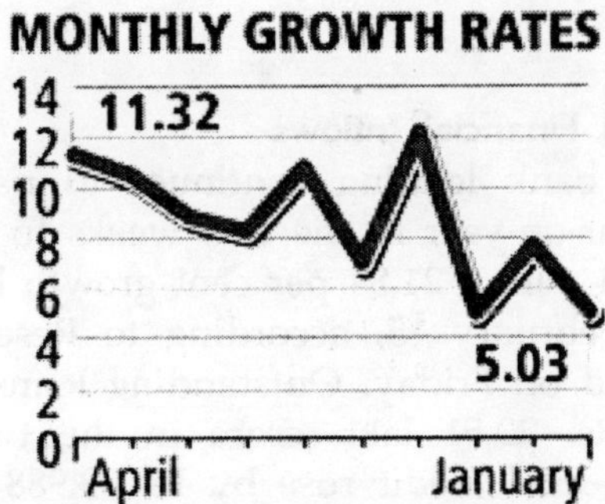

IIP at 5.3%

Sector	*2007-Jan. (% growth)*	*2008-Jan. (% growth)*	*Overall Apr.-Jan. 2006-07 (% growth)*	*Overall Apr.-Jan. 2007-09 (% growth)*
Mining	7.7	1.8	4.8	4.6
Manufacturing	12.3	5.9	12.1	9.2
Electricity	8.3	3.3	7.6	6.3
Overall	11.6	5.3	11.2	8.7

Source: Central Statistical Organisation

Data on the Index of Industrial Production (IIP) were released by the Central Statistical Organisation at noon and caused the Bombay Stock Exchange's benchmark 30-scrip Sensex to plunge and close only 4.83 points up after advancing nearly 560 points at opening on the back of a global rally.

Inflation

India's inflation unexpectedly accelerated to a nine-month high at the beginning of March, making it more difficult for the central bank to reduce interest rates in an attempt to respond to slowing economic growth. Wholesale prices rose 5.11 per cent in the week ended March 1 from a year earlier, faster than the previous week's 5.02 per cent, according to the Ministry of Commerce and Industry in New Delhi on Friday.

Bank Lending and Financial Inflows

Meanwhile bank lending continues to rise, being up 21.88 per cent year-on-year in the two weeks to February 29, 2008, as compared with a 21.84 per cent growth logged in the fortnight ended February 15, according to Reserve Bank of India data released on Friday. Outstanding loans rose by Rs. 41,481 crore to Rs. 22.51 lakh crore in the two weeks to February 29. Non-food credit rose by Rs 39,988 crore to Rs. 22.07 lakh crore over the two weeks, while food credit rose by Rs. 1,493 crore to Rs. 44,311 crore in the same period. Deposits were up 23.7 per cent in the two weeks to February 29 from a year earlier. Banks' deposits rose by Rs. 43,539 lakh crore to Rs. 30.81 lakh crore.

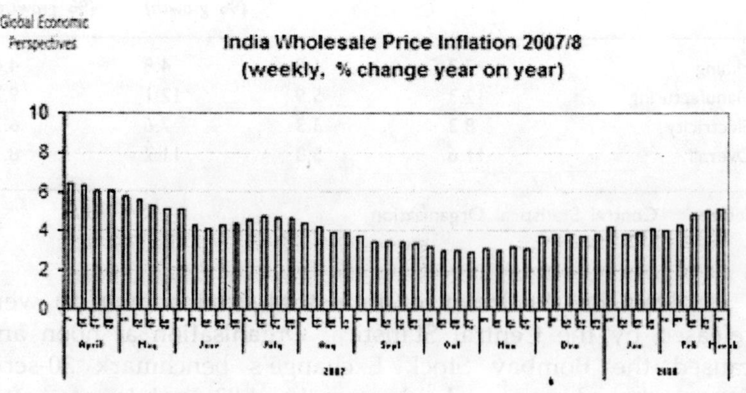

Source: India Ministry of Commerce and Industry.

At the same time the country's foreign-exchange reserves continued their upward march and increased by $2.2 billion in the week ended March 7 to $303.5 billion, the central bank said.

The Weakening Rupee (after appreciation of 12 per cent in 2007)

One of the greatest incognita on the India macro economic horizon at the present time is the future path of the rupee. The rupee has been weakening steadily over the last couple of months, and has fallen more than two per cent against the dollar so far this year (at the same time, it will be remembered that the dollar is also falling quite substantially). Conventional explanation of this movement are the pressure produced on the currency by equity outflows and a severe shortage of spot dollars in the market. India's Sensex, which has been Asia's worst-performing major benchmark index so far this year, fell 1.4 percent again last week, declining for a second week in a row after industrial production growth slowed in January, a reflection the higher interest rates are having on demand for consumer durables. Rising credit defaults in global stock markets have also had an impact on Indian stocks.

Curbs on foreign borrowing imposed by the government last year and the global credit woes caused by the US sub-prime crisis have also reduced the appetite for Indian equities. After gaining more than 12 per cent in 2007, the rupee has fallen steadily in 2008, and is now around 40.5 per dollar, its weakest level since mid-September and well off the near 10-year high of 39.16 reached in November.

All these current indicators raises doubts whether economy will grow at 9 per cent in FY 2008.

CHALLENGES

The country's achievements have, however, created new challenges. Some of the most prominent are:

I. Making Growth More Inclusive

Globalisation, liberalising reforms of the 1990s, shift of

governmen's focus away from the Agriculture and political conditions has resulted in virtual creation of 2 Indias viz. India (Urban, skilled and developed states) and Bharat. (rural, unskilled and backward states). Inequality can have huge social costs, and evidence of social unrest in some disadvantaged regions is growing. Food, clothing and shelter, now comprise a much smaller proportion of aggregate private final consumption expenditure than it did in 1990-91.

Food consumption expenditure has come down from 50 per cent to 40 per cent. Although in rural sector it is neary 55 per cent.

It has meant that the vast majority of the working population in the country has been unable to participate in the growth story, because their purchasing power has been under severe pressure.

Agriculture

Since the advent of liberalisation in 1990's this sector has been fairly ignored. As the Economic Survey (2008-09) has pegged the agricultural growth figures at a dismal 2.6 percent this year, despite favorable environmental parameters,. This will pull down the overall GDP (gross domestic product) growth. Declining investments, unchanging food production, declining agricultural growth is a cause for great concern. It sustains some two-thirds of India's population. Current agricultural practices are neither economically nor environmentally sustainable. A gradual degradation of natural resources through overuse and inappropriate use of chemical fertilizers has affected the soil quality resulting in stagnation in the yield levels poorly maintained irrigation systems coupled with changing climate adds up to the woes of the farmers. Lack of infrastructure and good extension services deny farmers' access to markets and negatively affect their profitability. Government of India has launched the National Food Security Mission and the Rashtriya Krishi Vikas Yojana to rejuvenate agriculture and improve farm income.

Employment and Poverty

While the services sector booms with promising job

opportunities for skilled workers, some 90 per cent of India's labor force remains trapped in low productivity informal sector jobs.

The 61st Round of NSSO Survey found that 47 million work opportunities were created during 1999-2000 to 2004-05, at an annual average of 9.4 million. Employment growth accelerated to 2.6 per cent during this period. The labour force, however, grew at 2.8 per cent per year, 0.2 per cent point faster than the workforce, resulting in an increase in the unemployment rate to 8.3 per cent in 2004-05 from 7.3 per cent in 1999-2000.

The proportion of persons below the poverty line declined from around 36 per cent of the population in 1993-94 to 28 per cent in 2004-05.

Divided States of India

India's higher-income states (Southern, Western and north-western States) have moved at a faster pace and successfully reduced poverty. India's poorer (BIMARU) states—Bihar, Madhya Pradesh Assam Rajasthan, Orissa, Uttar Pradesh, Chhattisgarh and Jharkhand, have lacked vision and are lagging behind mainly due to bad governance and political reasons.

2. Social Development and Governance

Differences in the quality of services delivery between Corporate and Government are now clearly visible. Large scale anomalies and corruption still plagues the administrative set-up. Hence, improper implementation of government's programs and as a result, poor delivery of core public services.

Education

Under 'Sarva Shiksha Abhiyan', India has made good progress in getting more children into primary school. But quality of education provided in government schools is way behind their private counterparts.

Health

There has been some improvement in the quality of health care over the years, but wide inter-State, male-female and rural-urban disparities in outcomes and impacts continue to persist. India's position on health parameters compared even to some of its neighbors continues to be unsatisfactory.

Various initiatives like The National Rural Health Mission (launched on April 12, 2005, to provide quality health services to the poorest households in the remotest rural regions. An Integrated Disease Surveillance Project (IDSP), AYUSH, Universal Immunization Programme, etc. has been taken by the government

But still delivery quality is a way behind their privately owned Hospitals and clinics.

Infrastructure

Rapid growth of the economy in recent years has created huge demand for good infrastructure. For urgently removing infrastructure supply constraints government has roped in private enterprises in this sector.

But, shortages are eroding the country's competitiveness and hurting the growth of labor-intensive enterprises, particularly export-oriented manufacturing which has the potential to absorb India's fast-growing working population

3. Accelerated and Sustaining Growth

Maintaining high growth will also require attention to some basics:

Fiscal Deficit

India has improved its fiscal indicators recently through the enactment of the Fiscal Responsibility and Budget Management Act (FRBMA), 2003. The fiscal deficit of the Centre as a proportion of GDP came down from 5.9 per cent in 2002-03 to 3.4 per cent in 2006-07 and is estimated to further decline to 3.3 per cent in 2007-08. States have been doing it better. Further improvements will be needed to create the space to fund the country's large infrastructure needs and ambitious social development programs.

Trade Deficit

The trade deficit is large and has widened due to high oil prices and increased non-oil imports. But due to ever growing FDIs, FIIs, NRI deposits, ECBs and services exports Forex reserves has increased. The excessive liquidity and appreciating rupee has become difficult to manage.

Reform

Reforms to address the basic constraints to growth is essential to should be done with a humane face. Reforms in India mainly depend on the political will of the elected government at the center or out of external/internal compulsions. The pace of reforms has been slower in the last year.

RECOMMENDED STRATEGY FOR ACCELERATED AND INCLUSIVE GROWTH (WITH A SPECIAL FOCUS TO AGRICULTURE)

India cannot grow without Bharat. Economic disparities need to be bridged substantially in order to achieve the real inclusive growth. Creation of *One India* should be the objective.

A long-term strategic framework with better integration of all the sectors needs to be prepared for sustained economic growth. This system should be dynamic and flexible enough to respond to drastic changes in the Global scenario.

Agriculture

Management and Administrative Set-up

First of all, creation of Special autonomous expert body that would regulate agricultural and allied sectors(viz. Plantation, Water Resources, rural employment, Animal husbandry, Environment, Land, Food Processing and Food Security Management is required. It will act as a dynamic Integrator and implementer of the Strategies formulated for optimizing the limited resources in the desired time frame. It will co-ordinate with all the external and internal agencies (ministries, state government, etc.). Hence ample executionary, financial and regulatory powers need to be vested in it.

It will forecast, decide and recommend what, when, where and how to produce.

As the land and water resources is limited. Hence keeping in view of the food security, water resources, soil-type, profitability of farmers and Global food prices the type of crops and the area of land needs to be chosen.

Land and Farming

The co-operative or corporate farming needs to be encouraged for consolidating highly fragmented farm holdings and optimization of resources.

Land reform process needs to be sped up with computerization of all land holdings. Land Banks (with the readily available of data about lands' quality) needs to be created. The best quality of fertile lands should not be sacrificed for industrialisation/SEZs, etc. any other cost.

The less profitable crops and the shortfall thereof needs to be imported and subsidized (if needed). For example, a partial substitution of water intensive crops may be substituted by less water intensive and more profitable crops in places facing water shortage.

Water and Irrigation

Our farmers still rely heavily on the monsoon. Changing climatic condition due to Global warming has added to its uncertainties.

Water Resources is mostly unmanaged (scarcity and dwindling water table in most of the states and flood like situation in few states).

Setting up of IWRFC and 81 per cent increase in Irrigation outlay (in budget 2008-09) for AIBP (Accelerated Irrigation Benefit program), Rain-fed Area Development Program and micro irrigation projects is a welcome step. But distinct results are not yet visible. So, bottoms up approach of empowering local bodies at village and block level, in execution of these projects.

But finding ways of attracting massive private (national and global) investments has been a challenge.

Much hyped, 'Linking of national rivers' project during NDA government is still a distant dream.

Drinking Water

Increased allocation in RGDWM is helpful. But providing of drinking water should also be inter-linked with various ongoing and approved Irrigation and hydel power generation projects.

Seed

Best quality of seeds (developed indigenously or by foreign cos.) should be used for production in order to maximize production. Use of genetically improved seeds (sounds controversial) should be allowed after proper research.

Fertilizer

Encouragement of production and use of organic fertilizers viz. manures, compost, etc. by redirecting a chunk of subsidy given to chemical fertilizers. This will help in prevention of soil nutritional imbalance.

While Price mechanism of chemical Fertilizers need to be reworked. So that black marketers are completely eliminated and products are readily available for users. The subsidy should be passed on directly to the end consumer through the help of new technologies like mobile banking and bio-metric cards.

Rural Infrastructure

Good quality of roads, transportation and storage facilities, accessible 'mandis'(rural commodity market and drinking water with unabated supply of electricity, telephone and internet/broadband connectivity to all villages has become a necessity. This will be helpful for the farmers to get better deals for their produce, increase in output and better standard of living, in turn will reduce the migration pressure on the cities.

The Rural Housing schemes like Indira Awas Yojana should be extended to the landless families by redesigning the houses to low cost apartment types in order to save land for the future.

The increased allocation of 'Bharat Nirman' program for rural infrastructure this year is commendable but yet not sufficient. But still more funds through Public and private funding needs to roped in to further insulate our companies from global slowdown.

Social Development and Empowerment

Roping in private enterprises, Self Help Groups, communities, NGOs by giving fair incentives will be very fruitful for effective delivery of public services. For example, the Self-Employed Women's Association (SEWA), centered in Gujarat, has empowered hundreds of thousands of women through a myriad of small projects catering to health, elementary education and economic self-sufficiency by providing them small loans to start productive livelihoods. Companies like Hindustan Unilever and ITC (Indian Tobacco Company), among others, have long had distribution networks into village India, providing some investment, goods and services in areas beyond the government's reach. Particularly encouraging are joint ventures such as those between SEWA and ITC. Corporate muscle multiplies the benefits that civil society can bring to rural India.

Pricing and Marketing

Allowing direct buying from farms/village markets by large retail chains and companies will eliminate intermediaries will be a 2 way gain to both and benefits may be passed on to consumers also. Changes in Agricultural Produce Marketing Committees (APMC) Act (which makes the 'mandi' a monopoly controlled by local political interests), will free poor and exploited farmers from moneylenders' clutches.

Minimum support prices for key cereals decided by the Government should take into consideration the opportunity cost of procuring it from abroad and its production cost. This is important for the farmers' sustainability. India's awkwardly named

Food Processing

India being 2nd largest producer of fruits and

vegetables but less than 2 per cent of the production is processed.

This provides us a great opportunity for growth for employment generation. Replication of successful models like Amul, Dhara, operation flood needs to be done in various zones.

Special Agricultural Zones

In the light of above mentioned factors creation of 'Special Agricultural zones' on the lines of SEZ's will be of immense boost to development of food processing (including marine, fisheries and meat products), handicraft, textile industries and decreasing Exports.

Finance

Short term aspirin-type of populist solutions envisaged by FM in this year's budget like loan waiver, electricity waiver, etc. may help a bit to give a temporary relief and consumption boost. But it may fail to address the situation and its ramifications may negatively affect other sectors of the country. Interest rates should be lowered further.

Rural Credit inflows need to be increased manifolds. Short-term Rural Cooperative Credit Structure needs to be revamped. Allow 100 FDI in green-field rural-agricultural banks. Allow 51 per cent FDI in rural insurance covering health, weather and such insurance. Instead, NABARD should be more appropriately funded to pro-actively promote (private partnership), regulate and oversee micro-financing initiatives for providing enough credit to small farmers and village entrepreneurs in co-ordination with other Financial Institutions like RRB's, co-operatives and Banks. Let it decide the mode of financial instruments suited best for a particular region and prevailing situation. Questions like, whether to provide insurance covers to farm crops, plantation and animal resources or give adequate compensation according to the prevailing situations like failed crop or 'bird flu" kind of epidemic situations.

Timely intervention will greatly reduce the worries of the farmers. Increased penetration and availability of funds for Micro-financing activities (taking a lesson from

Bangladesh) by Self Help Groups (SHG run by Professionally Managed Groups) at grassroots' level will make the small and landless farmers to become more self reliant and keep away the 'mahajans' (loan sharks).

Investment

Investment in Agriculture, water management/ irrigation and rural infrastructure needs to be stepped up.

Huge government spending in developing rural infrastructure (roads, electrification, e-chaupals, cold-storages/ mobile banking/ATMs, etc.) and irrigation projects and the active participation of the Corporate with a limited exposure to Foreign Direct Investments is necessary. This could be one of the most potent driver for Indian growth engine and biggest employment generator.

Technology

Its one of the most decisive tool for optimization of the output as other resources are limited. So, for bringing in new technology in food processing, irrigation and farming, even 100 per cent FDIs may be invited.

Energy

Innovative use of non-conventional energy resources like sun, water, wind, etc. should be emphasized for electricity generation, irrigation and provision of drinking water through PPP.

Fresh impetus needs to be given for Bio-diesel and ethanol producing plants like Jatropha, sugarcane with the help of private companies to minimize import of growing oil import.

Information Technology

Information Technology is necessary for the effective implementation of all these above mentioned proposals

Introduction of multipurpose Bio-metric/smart cards for all rural residents is necessary for direct monitoring of various development schemes, plugging out the loopholes in PDS, reimbursement of employment guarantee schemes (like JRY, NREGP), housing schemes (Indira Vikas), loan waiver schemes, etc. and effective data (land, population, finance) collection.

Rural internet-enabled Information centres like e-chaupals (by ITC) has become a multipurpose growth tool for the villagers. These may in future be used as trading, banking as well as e-governance and training tool.

Government has proposed to establish such 100,000 broadband centers and a scheme for State Wide Area Network (SWAN) and State Data Centers with Rs. 800 crores this year.

For this year we need to rope in at least 50,000 crores (through tax/non-tax revenue, non-debt capital receipts and bonds) for e-governance and IT infrastructure initiatives. This will provide immensely required support for our badly hit star performers (IT cos.) due to US stagflation and stronger rupee.

Strategies for Other Sectors and Key Issues

In the light of changed global economic scenario its high time to go for radical reforms to make India grow at accelerated pace.

Create special Task force and economic packages for BIMARU (laggard states).

Privatize coal (old as well as new) mines sector and sell old oilfields to private companies for enhanced.

Decontrol sugar, fertilizer and pharmaceutical segments.

Allow 49 per cent FDI in all other insurance sector.

Enact a new bankruptcy law to enable quick exit or management change of sick enterprises.

Allow foreign equity in all retail trade, and 100 per cent FDI in branded specialty chains.

Open up the distribution of electricity to more private companies through credible cross subsidies.

Allow large private companies to run Transport systems and Metros.

Set-up new nuclear super power projects. Permit corporate investment in nuclear power. So, it's beneficial for going ahead with the 123 nuclear agreement with the US.

To absorb large inflows of foreign capital, amounting to

4 per cent of GDP (cost of sterilizing foreign inflows at Rs. 8,200 crore) means accelerating infrastructure and skill development so that foreign inflows can be converted productively into additional investment. Establish professional Autonomous body "Higher Education Regulatory Authority of India" to facilitate smooth introduction of contemporary courses (keeping in view of the Industry requirements) and regulating the standard of higher education provided by private and public institutes.

Recognize the certification of skill development, provided by the private Companies and Institutes.

Allow the Corporate to run the management of public health care and sanitation systems.

Sell minimum 10 per cent in Navratnas and other PSU's to public in order to finance rural development and infrastructure projects.

Push for labor reforms as the existing labor laws do not protect "workers and families," but only protect those workers with protected jobs. A new legislation balanced view is necessary to protect the interests of the unorganized labor force and end the caste and gender biases.

. Amend the Factories Act to extend the workweek from 48 hours to 60, and increase the daily working hours limit to 12 hours, to facilitate peak use of labour in seasonal industries.

For controlling down the inflationary pressure, we need to focus on the measures for removing supply-side bottle necks.

Off-budget borrowing (especially for oil and fertilizer) is entirely for subsidizing consumption, not for investment, and so constitutes the worst sort of Revenue deficit. It should be prevented.

Political Reforms

It has become clearly evident that in the last decade, rise of regional parties has weakened the government at the centre. They have been dictating terms to the government and adversely affect the government policies. This in turn, has affected the economy and state of Indian citizen.

So, the 2 strong national parties (BJP and Congress)

should sink their differences in larger interest of the country. Best option is to form a collaborative National Government or at least provide issue based support to each other's Government and keep the minority parties at bay to dictate their terms.

CONCLUSION

Pushing up radical reforms always requires a strong political will as it challenges the interests of privileged groups.

It may not show the results immediately. Long term benefits have been evident. It's always easier to push for reforms while being on the top of the growth ride rather than in the bottom of it. Delay will only increase the costs and complexities, further.

In the wake of Global Slowdown, India must look inwards and lead the World 'World Guru'.

References

Economic Survey of India (2007-08).

11th Five Year Plan (2007-12).

Kuznets, Simon, Modern Economic Growth: Rate, Structure, and Spread, New Haven: Yale University Press, 1966.

Asian Development Bank, "The Financial Crisis in Asia," Manila: Asian Development Bank, 1999.

Economic Times

Business Standard

Business World

www.ibef.org

www.wikepedia.org

www.worldbank.org

www.indiaeconomywatch.blogspot.com

www.pgpblogworldbank.org

www.macrosan.org

www.planningcommission.nic.in

www.iimc.in

www.indiabudget.nic.in

9

Inclusive Growth and Economic Development: Challenges and Prospects

R.U. Singh and Sangeeta

INTRODUCTION

Inclusive growth as dealt with in our 11th Plan means not excluding any section of the society. The aim is to have a fast and inclusive growth of the entire economy. The benefits of development should reach all. Inclusiveness has four attributes opportunity, capability, access and security. Consistent with this definition, inclusive growth is a process in which economic growth, measured by a sustained expansion in GDP contributes to an enlargement of the scale and scope of all four dimensions. The relationship between inequality and exclusiveness/inclusiveness, income enters the picture primarily through the opportunity dimension. However, income is the result of an opportunity being exploited. It depends on a number of factors including the motivation and performance of the individual himself. In this sense it is unreasonable to hold the growth or the development process itself entirely accountable for the result. The effectiveness of the process is realised when a large number of people get legitimate opportunities to earn income. Capability dimension relates to education and skill creation. The eleventh plan aims to provide the means for people to create or enhance there capabilities in order to exploit available opportunities. There are three essential components to any educational process. It must provide a basic set of skills that the individual needs to function within his socio-economic environment.

They are literacy, numeric and IT capabilities. It is the duty of the government to provide security to the people. 'Access' this term encompasses both opportunity and capability in the sense of people having access to job and education. It is essential that the demand for labour 'human capital' with its supply. India is rapidly growing economy and turbulent one. Sectors and companies merge, emerge.

Overall growth trend of an economy is the prerequisite of development of any state or country, the high and sustained growing trend in its GDP for a long period provides the necessary wherewithals for building business confidence, the economic tools of analysis have gained a wide application to the process of decision-making, possibly because modern business problems are so complex that decision-makers personal experience, institution, insight, foresight and judgment alone are no longer adequate. To provide an appropriate solution to complex business problems, the applications of economic tools and logic to the business problems, not only reveals the behavioural pattern of economic entities and variables involved in business problems but also helps in arriving at an optimum solution to the problem.

The approach paper to Eleventh Five Year Plan starts with the assertion that the Indian economy on the eve of the 11th Plan is in a much stronger position that it was a few years ago. After slowing down to an average growth rate of about 5.5 per cent in the Ninth Plan period (1997-98 to 2001-02), it has accelerated in recent years and the average growth rate in the Tenth Plan period (2002-03 to 2006-07) is likely to be about 7 per cent. This is below the Tenth Plan target of 8 per cent, but it is the highest growth rate achieved in any plan period. While this performance reflects the strength of the economy in many areas, it is also true that large parts of our population are still to experience a decisive improvement in their standard of living. The percentage of the population below the poverty line is declining, but only at a modest pace. Far too many people still lack access to basis services such as health, education, clean drinking water and sanitation facilities without which they cannot be empowered to claim their share in the benefits of growth. These problems are more severe in some states than in others, and in general they are especially severe in rural areas.

This paper proposes to tackle the issue of inclusive growth.

Regional Disparities

A great impediment in the way of inclusive growth are the regional disparities visible in almost all parts of the country. Few states like Gujarat, Punjab, Maharashtra, Tamil Nadu, etc. are at the pinnacle of development whereas apart from several middle-rung, BIMARU states like Bihar, MP, Rajasthan, UP, etc. are languishing at the bottom of the ladder.

The disparities is income are intrastate as well as interstate. This is true of poverty levels also. Infrastructure is severely constrained and other problems include bad fiscal management, widespread agriculture sector problems, unemployment, etc. The measure to reduce regional disparities include investment in less developed states for higher growth and reduction in poverty, prudent fiscal management, focus on reducing population, agricultural sector reforms, following regionally diversified strategies, emphasis on technologies, productive employment, should be generated, social sector performance and social inclusion should be improved. Now we reach at the policy suggestions for achieving inclusive growth:

First, equity matters for development. It is important for its own sake for higher growth. There is no trade-off between growth and equity. If we define equity in terms of empowerment and increase in participation of the poor.

Second, agricultural development should be given

priority for more inclusive growth. Steeping up agricultural growth is essential for reducing poverty. Land issues, irrigation and water management, credit research and extension, marketing, etc. have to be improved in the next decade to improve agricultural growth. Third, there is need to have macro-poor policies for inclusive growth. In terms, fiscal policy pro-poor approach involves increasing tax/GDP ratio, improving expenditure on social sector, agriculture and rural development, infrastructure and other capital expenditures.

Monetary policy should contain inflation particularly food prices also reduce spread between lending and deposit rates. Pro-poor trade liberalisation and exchange rate policies are needed to promote employment to labour intensive exports and also measures to reduce volatility in prices due to globalisation.

Third, priority should be given to the policies that improve quantity and quality of employment growth. Priority to public investment in physical (irrigation, trade, communication, transport, electricity, etc.) and human infrastructure (health, education, etc.) is considered one of the important factors responsible for inclusive growth. Also priority to rapid growth in agriculture and several non-farm sector are important for poverty reduction.

Fourth, structural change in economy should follow agriculture-industry-service sequence. In GDP shares, India jumped from agriculture to services without concentrating on manufacturing. The share of employment in manufacturing in Malaysia is 50 per cent, in Korea 62 per cent, in China 31 per cent whereas it is not even 15 per cent in India. Therefore, there is a need to develop industry in order to improve employment. Jumping to services is not the solution. High agriculture growth of 4 per cent and industry growth of more than 10 per cent are needed for better structural change. In India, growth acceleration has been significant in service sectors. But importance should have been given first to agriculture and then to manufacturing, rural infrastructure, etc. in the reforms for better employment, income and equity.

Fifth, equalities of opportunities is important. Even if we don't follow equitable distribution of assets, everyone should get equal opportunity for better education and health. Presently, the Indian economy is on a high growth track. While the Indian government has implemented policies that unleashed the country's growth potential, it should also embark on a process of social transformation that ends discrimination on the basis of caste, class and gender. We also need to pay more attention to provide clean water, access to health care and high quality education. A sustained emphasis on education and health are needed in the next decade in many states for inclusive growth.

Sixth, South East Asian and East Asian experience shows that globalisation with better initial conditions have increased employment and incomes for workers and led to equitable development. India should learn from China on agricultural growth, rural non-farm employment, public investment and human development. China, on the whole, has done better than India on the inclusive growth front because she had better initial condition and reforms work better in more egalitarian society.

Seventh, development of technology is important for inclusive growth. The spread of green revolution in poorer states in India shows its potential for reducing regional disparities in development. Other prospects include propagation of biotechnology and IT. Then there is lot of knowledge gap in agriculture. Even with existing technology, productive can be improved.

Eighth, the process of reforms can now be shifted to more efficient delivery systems of public services. Better governance is very important for inclusive development.

Infrastructural Disparities

The Eleventh Finance Commission devised an infrastructure index for the states for the year 1999. The index brings out a composite comparative profile of the availability of physical, social and institutional infrastructure in the states.

Among all the states that existed in 1999, Goa had the highest infrastructure index, i.e., it was the best placed state in terms of infrastructure facilities while Arunachal Pradesh had the lowest infrastructure index.

Disparities in the Growth of Gross State Domestic

Product Mr. Montek S. Ahluwalia, in his paper 'Economic Performance of the State in the Post-Reforms Period' has analysed the disparities in the growth performance of different states.

Rural-Urban Disparities

There has always existed an urban—rural divide in terms of development. But this divide has widened after the independence during the planning era. The ratio of urban income to rural income which was just about 1.6 in 1951 and continued to remain within reasonable limit during the first three decades of development planning managed to reach 2.1 in 1980-81 and worsened during the last two decades to record a level close to 4.5 large and medium cities are growing but the rural areas are still highly neglected in the growth process and are experiencing economic stagnation. The national income statistics shows a decline of the share of agriculture to about 15 per cent of GDP but the share of population dependent on agriculture remains the same. The marginal farmers, the small farmers and the landless labour experience hardship due to the negligence surrounding the agricultural sector in today's globalised economic.

Rural agricultural distress is evident in the suicide committed by the farmers. As also in the increase in the naxalism which is basically a development problem. More than one-fourth of the Indian district have been declared as naxalite-affected area by the Ministry of Home Affairs. The latest report on the Chhattisgarh adivasis plight have shown the effect of a neglected rural population taking solace in the naxalite camps. The guillible dalits, adivasis, the unemployed, the poor and the illiterate rural mass in lured by the camps on the assurance of justice. The oppressive and the exploitive behaviour of the rural moneyed class and the in effective government machinery has also given impetus to the conversion of the ignorant mass who again are assured of employment and monetary gains.

India has experienced an balanced growth where some cities are growing on all fronts and some rural and semi-urban areas are experiencing retrogression. The same trend is evident in the urban areas where the disparity is more

Table I

Index of Social and Economic Infrastructure, 1991

(Arranged in Increasing Order)

S. No.	*States*	*Index*
1.	Arunachal Pradesh	69.71
2.	Jammu and Kashmir	71.46
3.	Tripura	74.87
4.	Manipur	75.39
5.	Meghalaya	75.49
6.	Rajasthan	75.86
7.	Nagaland	76.14
8.	Madhya Pradesh	76.79
9.	Assam	77.72
10.	Orissa	81.00
11.	Bihar	81.33
12.	Mizoram	82.13
13.	Himachal Pradesh	95.03
14.	Uttar Pradesh	101.23
15.	Andhra Pradesh	103.30
16.	Karnataka	104.88
17.	Sikkim	108.99
18.	West Bengal	111.25
19.	Maharashtra	112.80
20.	Gujarat	124.31
21.	Haryana	137.54
22.	Tamil Nadu	149.10
23.	Kerala	178.68
24.	Punjab	187.57
25.	Goa	200.57

Source: Eleventh Finance Commission Report, 2000.

evident in the form of emergence of large slum areas who live a life of destitute and also is seen in the low wages rampant unemployment, semi-employment and under-employment. Most of the mineral wealth of the country is in the tribal belt, mining and other developmental activities like power and irrigation projects often lead to large scale displacement of tribals from their habitats. Often, they are not properly rehabilitated economically, socially and culturally.

Indeed, they have often been victims of development process. Even after the implementation of ten five year plans the regional disparity still remains a major issue. In Indian context focus is on government interference through policies and resource allocation. Different regions vary in resources, hence India's planned development strategy brings about a lop sided growth. There are low performing regions which are related to its inadequate capital formation indebted agriculture and lack proper infrastructure. In these regions, cycle of stagnation and poverty has continued the economic reforms has aggravated the situation further by directing the flow of domestic and foreign investment towards better performing regions. The low performing regions already suffer from weak organisation of economic institutions, hence inclusive growth process should involve development strategy with major thrust on fast human capital development, agricultural modernization and rural industrialisation. In the present era of globalisation empirical study indicate the concentration of wealth in a few hands which further worsens the disparity. While corporate profits in the national income is increasing manifold the wage level is experiencing a declining trend of the total wages distributed the share of the top management is in the up rise the high salary of the CEO's had become a topic of much debate in the investment capital deprived economy like India. English speaking and computer literate graduates have also captured a substantial employment opportunities. According to the Asian Development Banks study widening differentials in earnings of the college educated *vis-à-vis* less educated individual appear to be one of the major factors responsible for increasing income inequality in India. The extremely non-inclusive nature of the recent economic growth in India can be attributed to the very poor human development specially in rural areas.

Industrial Growth Disparities

The initial distribution of industries in India was determined by the historical process of growth in the interests of the British rulers. As a result, most of the industries got concentrated at a few centres. This pattern continued in the post-Independence period as well. For instance, a study of 28 large-scale manufacturing industries in India in 1950 showed the dominance of the Western region and West Bengal in the regional distribution of industries. Thus, 34.60 per cent of total productive capital was concentrated in West Bengal, their combined share being as much as 59.25 per cent. Taken together, the Western region and West Bengal accounted for 63.03 per cent of total persons employed, 60.41 per cent of gross ex-factory value of output, and 63.95 per cent of value added by manufacturer.

This pattern of concentration has not changed substantially during the planning period despite all attempts made at regional dispersal of industries. For instance, as late as 2002-03 the two States of Maharashtra and Tamil Nadu accounted for 28.9 per cent of factory employment, 28.5 per cent of invested capital, 28.8 per cent of gross output and 29.1 per cent of value added by manufacture. If the three industrially advanced States of Maharashtra, Gujarat and Tamil Nadu are considered together, the true picture of regional concentration of industries is explicitly brought into prominence. In 2002-03 these three States together (having 20.4 per cent of total population according to 2001 census) accounted for 45.0 per cent of gross output, 42.4 per cent of value added, 45.7 per cent of total invested capital, and 37.9 per cent of employment in factory sector. The mere fact that more than two-fifths of the total output, value added and fixed capital and a little less than two-fifths of total employment in factory sector is found in these three States alone while the remaining States and Union Territories contribute only a little more than half of total value added and total output is a proof of substantial regional concentration of industries in the three industrially advanced States of Maharashtra, Gujarat and Tamil Nadu.

Agricultural Disparity

Agriculture is by far the dominant sector as far as total employment generation is concerned. It also contributes about 20 per cent to the GDP. But most distressingly, in the last decade, growth rate in agriculture was less than 2 per cent per annum.

So what ware the challenges for reaching 4 per cent growth in agriculture? The supply and demand side constraints have to be removed to raise overall growth in agriculture. There are basically four issues that need to be focused:

(a) land and water management
(b) research and extension
(c) inputs including credit
(d) marketing including price policy

Appropriate infrastructure and institutions are needed to focus on all these issues. Speedy implementation of Bharat Nirman is needed for creating rural infrastructure. Subsidy reduction should not be linked to resource mobilisation. It should be linked more with sustainability of natural resources and cropping patterns. The government plans to have second Green Revolution by diversifying agriculture in crop sector and allied activities.

CHALLENGES

The major challenges the 11th Five Year Plan's approach paper points out are:

(i) Providing Essential Public Services for the Poor

The most important challenge is how to provide essential public services such as education and health to large parts of our population who are denied these services at present.

(ii) Regaining Agricultural Dynamism

One of the major challenges of the 11th Plan must be to reverse the deceleration in agricultural growth from 3.2 per cent observed between 1980 and 1996-97 to a trend average of only 1.5 per cent subsequently. This deceleration is undoubtedly at the root of the problem of rural distress that has surfaced in many pats of the country. A second green revolution is urgently needed to raise the growth rate of agricultural GDP to around 4 per cent.

(iii) Increasing Manufacturing Competitiveness

The manufacturing sector has also not grown as rapidly as might have been expected. The average growth rate of this sector has accelerated compared to the Ninth Plan but is unlikely to exceed 8 per cent in the 10th Plan. It should be targeted to grow at around 12 per cent or so if we want to achieve a GDP growth of between 8 and 9 per cent. The most important constraint in achieving a faster growth of manufacturing is the fact that infrastructure, consisting of roads, railway, ports, airports communication and electric power, is not up to the standards prevalent in our competitor countries. This must be substantially rectified within the next 5-10 years if our enterprises are to compete effectively.

(iv) Developing Human Resource

To ensure a continuous and growing supply of quality investment in public sector institutions of higher learning combined with fundamental reforms of the curriculum and also service conditions to attract high quality faculty. The scope for expanding capacity through private sector initiatives in higher learning must also be fully exploited, while also ensuring that quality standards are not diluted. Unless this is done on an urgent basis, we will fail to attain global standards.

(v) Protecting the Environment

Environmental concerns are growing globally as well as within the country. Neglect of environmental considerations can lead to adverse effects very quickly. The threat of climate change also posses real challenges to the well-being of future generations which we can ill afford to ignore. Our development a strategy has to be sensitive to these growing concerns and should ensure that these threats and trade-offs are appropriately evaluated.

CONCLUSIONS

Improvement in basic infrastructural facilities like power, transport, telecommunication and irrigation in backward states is a precondition to improve the quality of life of people and to usher in sustainable development in them. Availability of assured power supply, developed transport system and modern telecommunication facilities are important factors to attract private investments into these states.

The investment in agriculture needs to be stepped up especially in the lagging regions. The backward and forward linkages of agriculture in poorer regions need to be emphasised more. Investment in water harvesting, soil conservations, rural roads, warehouses, processing activities and promotion of high value crops should be emphasises. Since agricultural growth is found to be more disparate, steps to equalise it will certainly reduce the regional imbalances.

The governments of backward states are fiscally weak and lack resources. Liberalisation process and various reforms have further weakened their financial position. It is hoped that resources flows to the states via Finance Commission awards and Planning Commission dispensation will continue and are likely to remain positively discriminating in favour of backward states. In fact, according to Rao (2000), these transfers are found to be progressive in reducing regional disparities. However, direct public sector investment by the central government in the states are likely to dry up gradually due to severe budged constraint of the Centre. Under the above circumstances, an important factor that influences the speed of economic progress of a state is the quality of governance. A better administered state is more efficient in raising revenues and putting them to better use. They are the states, which will attract more private investment both from domestic and foreign sources. Such states are also in a position to prepare viable projects and successfully bid central assistance of external funding. Hence, governance needs to be given immediate attention, especially in the backward states.

Service sector has been found to be the new driver of the growth process. Especially, the banking and insurance sector and infrastructure have contributed to acceleration of many states. There is a need to promote these sectors on priority, in backward regions.

References

Misra, S.K. and Puri, V.K., 2006, Economics of Development and Planning, Himalaya Publishing House, New Delhi.

Papola, T.S., Reducing Imbalances in Regional Development: An Essential Ingredient of Strategy for "Inclusive Growth". Inaugural address at the National Seminar on "Making Growth Inclusive with Special Reference to Imbalances in Regional Development", Department of Economics, University of Jammu, Jammu, 12-13 March, 2007.

Planning Commission (October 2006), Approach paper to the Eleventh Five Year Plan (2007-12), Government of India, New Delhi.

Ravallion, Martin (2000), "What is Needed for a Pro-poor Growth Process in India?", *Economics and Political Weekly*, March.

S. Mahendra Dev, "Regional Disparities in poverty and Malnutrition, paper presented at a Seminar at ISID, New Delhi, September 16-18, 2005.

Singh, R.K. (2004), *Economic Reforms in India* (ed.), Abhijeet Publications, New Delhi.

10

India: Economic Growth and Pattern of Distribution

SANJAY KUMAR

INTRODUCTION

Amidst a global polemic, all the world over, the Indian economists and social scientists of various disciplines have been confronting—having being divided into two broad groups—against each other to justify and oppose the pattern of economic development strategy of India under the aegis of globalisation and liberalisation. This Polemic between the two segments of academicians, diametrically opposed to each other, has stretched widely, embracing the entire areas, economic, political, social and cultural too, but the object of this paper is to examine whether the growth extends the benefits of development to the poorer collective, particularly, the unorganized sector of society. Let us have a cursory glance upon the economic scenario of India, which has, now, become an irreversible part of the world economy after being itself linked with globalisation.

The *Fobers,* a prestigious American journal has recently Published, after a close examination, a list of the millionaires in the world as entitled "The World's Richest people." This list is numerically comprised of 946 millionaires, and 26 among them are Indian. The most surprising is the fact that among them 178 millionaires have got place for the first time, with Russians 19, Indian 14, Chinese 13, and Spainish 10, besides one millionaire each from Cyprus, Oman, Rumania and Sarbia.

INCREASING NUMBERS OF MISSIONARIES

In the list of 2005 the total number of millionaires in the world accounted for 768 where as the 2006 list was comprised of altogether 946 millionaires. Consequently, the growth rate in millionaires has markedly received the pace of 23 percent but the same growth rate for India has been unprecedentedly high, approaching the level of 64 percent. Appraising this miraculous development in India the journal has joyfully commented the 20 years old Japanese economic dominance on Asia has evaporated, its supermacy regarding possession of highest number of millionaires has no longer remained intact. Now, Japan has slept from first position to second position, in comparison to India with total numerical strength of millionaires being 36 with their total capital aggregating to 191 million dollars. Now Japan comes next with its millionaires with 64 million dollar as their total capital. The Ambani brothers, (Anil Ambani and Mukesh Ambani) with Laxmi Mital have placed themselves among the 20 richest persons of the world, Luxmi Mital on 5th, Mukesh Ambani on 14th and Anil Ambani on 18th position. Among the 20, 5 are American, only two more than the Indian. On the 21st position again, one can see the Indian Azeem Prem Ji. Ratan Tata has launched his campaign to purchase iron and steel companies in the European countries. All these developments in India favouring the Indian corporate sector had enthused the *Times of India* to display on its front page on the occasion of New Year, 2007 about the world victory that was started by Indian Corporate Sector. In context of all these developments the *Abserver* from London had written that to go ahead has become the clarion call of India because the success under globalisation is knocking the doors of India. But in a comment of the same *Abserver* Amelia gentleman gave an opposite comment as he wrote that the bubbles of prosperity in Delhi or in the financial capital Bombay make us astonished when we go to a few miles away from them. Immediately the myth of being India emerging as a supper power immediately gets tarnished.

WHAT RED INDIA IS?

The moment one come out from the glass made skyscrapers, in which there are call centre's offices designed and named after American style the new India suddenly disappears; and in that stead there appeared a distinct India, diametrically opposed to what Delhi and Mumbai display. Out of these prosperous looking cities there exists an another India, with 70 percent of its population striving hard for their subsistances and depends on agriculture for their living, 30 crores people are forced to live below poverty line, peasants in ragged garments are seen on roads carrying torn bags loaded on bullock, minor, thin and weak children breaking stone chips to be used in road construction.

Immediately after the *Fobers* report there came the report of Planning commission whose command is in the hand of Montek Singh Ahalualia, a staunch supporter of trickle down Politics. In his many papers he has pleaded that government should no take any restrictive measures against growing inequality in income, because, in his arguments, with the acceleration of income and wealth of big business houses there would arise greater need for servants and some parts of income earned by big capital would, thus, be driven to their employees and the poverty of the poor people would be eliminated in due course. For him the market forces should be allowed to operate freely without any sort of interruption on the part of government.

OFFICIAL MYTHS

In the report of the Planning Commission published for 2004-05 there has been said that poverty in India has unintermittently been reducing. The population living below the poverty line was 36 percent in 1993-94, which has been reduced to 27.5 percent in 2004-05.[1] In an another estimation the percentage of the people living below poverty line in 1999-2000 was 26.1 which decelerated to 21.8 percent in 2004-05.[2] In both the reports there has been claimed that the Washington Common Consensus, based on globalisation, has benefited both the corporate sector, whose income and dividend have grown and the poor segment of society which has gradually been coming out from its poverty and deprivation. There has been argued that if this process of liberalisation is allowed to operate uninterruptedly, the poverty of the masses would be removed within a couple of years. Till people should wait patiently with hope that a golden time has to come after a few years and the sacrifice mode today would be very little incomparision to the prosperity that would be achieved in near future.

In the Polemic the adherents of globalisation take us back to the precept of Kuzuetz's curve, which symbolises that in modern development process increase in income disparity is an inevitable factor, but with the increasing growth rate the disparity gradually decelerate. This economic postulation was presented by Kuznetz from the presidential chair of American Economic Association through his speech captioned as "Economic growth and Income Inequality." In his hypothesis it was laid down that an agricultural economy proceeding towards industrial economy creates in its initial years income disparity, which, later on, under the speedy growth rate begins to make this disparity narrowed. His theory has been presented in the shape of a below shaped Roman alphabet 'n'. It was his this theory for which he was awarded with the Novel Prize in 1971. But all these formulation have been challenged as not being based on reliable sources.

The aforesaid economic theory is the basis relying upon which pro-globalisation forces acclaim the growth in GDP as an achievements scored by India under the aura of liberalisation. How much the claim for 9 percent growth in GDP since the last two years and 8.6 percent growth prior to it, is justified, has been examined by the *Economic and Political weekly*, in its editorial[3]. While evaluating the reasons responsible for this growth rate the paper has examined the leap in saving and investment figures and located two main reasons responsible for them. According to the assessment this leap appears to be due to sectoral saving and investment and secondly due to amendments introduced in 1999-2000 in NSS and changes in base year. This has been proved by the fact that the sector and areas, in which statistical changes were introduced, have registered the high growth. In its example citation, the paper has given certain examples: earlier the expenses incurred upon several public sector's welfare schemes like *Sarva Shiksha Abhiyan*, Mid-day meal, expenses on District Primary education, etc. were assimilated in consumer expenses but now all of them have been included in the list of capital expenses. Similarly the expenses on department's tools and machineries and expenses of new companies and the companies which are under the process of installation have also been included in capital expenses. It was not so earlier. These are the sectors in which huge expenses have been done in recent years. All these statistical mesmerisms have brought the growth rate to a colossal height.

ANOTHER SIDE OF THE COIN

On the another side there are other sectors where all these mesmerisms of growth appear to have miserably failed. For example, there is the agricultural sector, with which there are tagged the employment and subsistance of a huge masses. In spite of claimed 9 percent growth rate, the agricultural sector's growth rate is only 2.7 percent and its contribution to the GDP has been reduced to less than 20 percent. Besides it the two sectors, service sector and industry sector have registered a growth rate more than 10 percent. Consequently, with a low growth rate in agriculture the average rate of growth has an accelerated pace. In its simple analysis the only inference to be drawn is that the growth in India is being achieved by passing agricultural sector that is, in other words, the benefits of growth are not approaching villages and rural population. This is the tragedy of this growth, the 60 percent population residing in rural sector is not benefited by this growth process. According to the survey result of

NSSO, conducted for 1993-94 to 2004-05, the average annual reduction in poverty for 11 years was recorded as 0.74 percent while the growth of GDP was recorded at the rate of 9 percent annually. Even in the years between 1999-2000 and 2004-05 when the average annual rate of growth approached 7 to 8 percent the rate of poverty reduction was of 0.79 percent. In the same period there was registered 20 percent growth rate in millionaires. In a survey it was inferred that in the entire Asia-pacific region India scored top regarding the growth rate of millionaires. This pattern of growth is an explicit example of the fact that the achievement of growth is very unevenly distributed— benefiting the richer and leaving aside the poorer people.

REASONS FOR UNEVEN GROWTH

This uneven growth has been creating a wide ditch between not only poor and richer sectors of people but also among states and inside the states. The most surprising is the fact that on the economic strategy of India the World Bank has promulgated a country report in which it has been established that economic growth and economic disparity are *sin qua non* for development. If this logic is accepted, then the objective of employment generation and altering the condition of poor people have no relevances. In service sector where employment generation has taken place, the persons employed are forced to work for low paid wages without any social security, etc.

A second factor which is responsible for income inequality is the price policy of the government. The unintermittent growth in prices reduces the savings of common men and places them in the rank of poverty striken people. Globalisation and liberalisation have created conditions in which the both methods of government and the Central Bank of the government, qualitative and qualitative methods have become ineffective in restricting prices of commodities. All the qualitative methods like reduction in interest rate, withdrawal of money by government through sale of its bonds and shares, the methods of CRR, etc. and qualitative methods like order of the Central Bank (RBI) to commercial banks to reduce their credit for purchase of some particular items, etc. have become ineffective under liberalisation. Under liberalised economy the control of the Central Bank on the money has been ceased due to several reasons. The important reasons are the reduced control of Central Bank (RBI) on money issued by banks, expansion of non-banking credit, etc. The system of purchasing through credit cards, has considerably reduced the control of the Central Bank on the credit extension of commercial banks. This method of marketing through credit card has reduced the possibility for reducing demands of services or commodities by the application of banking policy.

In globalisation the restrictions on capital in and out flow have become irrelevant. In case of a county where banks raise interest rate on credit to control the supply of money for price reduction, immediately money from low interest rate countries will rush to fill the gap. In these circumstances the money deposit in commercial banks will increase because to have themselves benefited by the higher interest rate the foreign financers will rush to deposit their money in these banks. Consequently, the Central Bank, in spite of its all efforts, will fail to restrict price rise. Through *Hawala* and smuggling a huge amount of money has been coming in India. Consequently, the supply of money in Indian market has flooded itself and Central Bank is not in a position to control it.

Globalisation with its mechanism of liberalisation has thus widen the gaps between rich and poor.

Notes and References

1. "Evaluation of poverty", *A Report by the Planning Commission for 2004-05,* A Report by *Fobers,* the American Journal, March, 2007.
2. *Economic and Political Weekly,* 10 February, 2007, "Editorial".

Industrial Development Path of Less Developed Regions in the Globalised Economy

Special reference to North Eastern Regions of India

Tikendrajit Poonam and Jayanti Ningombam

The world economy has been undergoing unprecedented changes leading to emergence of market driven society. This has necessitated structural adjustment internationally as demanded by the forces influencing global business environment. The global village has been offering umpteen opportunities and challenges, concomitantly. As a result, the Indian industry has been addressing a profound changes in economic realities and policies throughout the world in 1990s. The changes have also pushed the Indian economy from the command economy into market economy which has been referred to as liberalisation and globalisation of the Indian economy. The long term objectives of such reforms were to make the economy make efficient and competitive by (1) replacing the inward looking growth strategy with an outward-oriented one, and (2) reducing the role of the state in the economy.

Here, it is believed that the reform process will lead to achieve—high rate of growth, enlargement of employment, reduction of population living below the poverty line, reduction of regional disparities between the rich and the poor states of India, etc. Even after completion of 15 years of reform process the NE region still remains in the back waters. It has aggravated the problem of poverty, unemployment and it has not only accentuated regional disparity but also intra-regional disparity among the states of the region.

The paper analyses the issues associated with industrial relocation in the era of globalisation with special reference to North Eastern Region of India. To be more specific the paper emphasizes the (i) review of the industrial development, (ii) discusses the causes of backwardness, (iii) focuses upon the potential areas for development of industry, and (iv) proposes a roadmap for the growth of industry to reap the opportunities of industrial relocation in the North Eastern Region of India.

INTRODUCTION

Globalisation, a buzz world is one of the most debated issues in recent times throughout the world. Their impacts in a developing country like India are immense. The term "Globalisation" has different meaning to different parties. It affects society at various dimensions—social, political, economic and cultural. In its economic dimension it implies a process of transnationalisation of production and capital standardization of consumer taste and their legitimization with the help of international bodies such as World Bank, International Monetary Fund and World Trade Organization. After independence India had introduce state control to facilitate towards liberalisation and privatization. This process in India began in 1991 unlike other countries where it started in the 1980. After completion of first generation reforms our country is now passing through the generation reforms were associated with industrial deregulation, opening the economy to trade, disinvestments and privatization, financial sector reforms and private financing of infrastructure. The second generation reforms are characterized by extending reforms to the states, labour legislation, the function of the legal system, bringing duty structure at the global standard, etc.

The impact of globalisation is experienced by most of the developing countries of the world. Globalisation has enabled India also to find a strong foothold in the world map. She has an impact on all aspect of the economy. But despite of the increase on GDP, export enhancement, import substitution, employment generation, increase in purchasing power, etc. there is unequal insurance of the benefits to the entire region.

In fact, the integrated new global market does not ensure equal benefits to all the state of India. Liberalised economy of India and its rapid growth does not provide equal benefit to all regions of the country. The North East which is the poorest and remotest part of the country is yet to enjoy significant share of the benefits of liberalised process due to one or other factors.

OBJECTIVES

The objective of the paper is to analyse the issues associated with industrial relocation in the era of globalisation with special reference to North Eastern Region of India. To be more specific the objects of the paper are to: (i) review of the industrial development, (ii) discuss the causes of backwardness, (iii) focus upon the potential areas for development of industry, and (iv) propose a roadmap for the growth of industry to reap the opportunities of industrial relocation in the North Eastern Region of India.

The North East Scenario

The North Eastern Region (NER) of India consisting of eight states viz., Assam, Arunachal Pradesh, Manipur, Meghalaya, Mizoram, Tripura and Sikkim has got its definite identity due to its peculiar physical economic and socio-cultural characteristics. The region covers an area of 2.26 lack sq. km. It accounts for 7.9 per cent of total geographical area of the country. With a population of 39 millions (2001), it accounts for 3.8 per cent of the total population of India. Their combined contribution to the national economy is 2 per cent. All the states in the North East regions are categorized as Special Category States. The lack of basic infrastructure like roads, non-availability of power inadequate social infrastructure and absence of avenues for creating employment opportunities are common to the states of this region. As the development of any economy is always associated with industrialisation, it is necessary to study the industrial scenario of NE here.

The Industrial Scenario of North East

Despite of 55 years of economic planning the region remains in the backwaters due to the existence of industrial backwardness. The industrial backwardness is reflected by the fact that the region's share in value added by manufacture is hardly 2 per cent and with 3.02 per cent of the existing SSI units. For having an idea of the development of an economy, one can emphasizes the process of setting up large and medium scale industries in the region which can be seen from Table 1.

TABLE I

Large and Medium Industries in NE Regions

Sl. No.	*Name of the State*	*No. of Units in 1993*	*Percentage 1993*	*No. of Units in 1999*	*Percentage 1999*
1.	Arunachal Pradesh	17	5.8	17	9.55
2.	Assam	118	74.8	129	72.48
3.	Manipur	6	3.9	12	6.74
4.	Meghalaya	7	4.5	10	5.62
5.	Mizoram	1	0.3	1	0.56
6.	Nagaland	16	10.4	7	3.93
7.	Tripura	1	0.3	2	1.12
	Total	166	100.00	178	100.00

Source: Basic Statistics of NER, Various issues, NEC, Shillong.

From the table it is seen that there are 178 large and medium scale industries in NER. In the year 1993 the figure was only 166. Among the NE states, Assam's share is 72.4 per cent. The share of other states is negotiable.

Considering the scheme of industrialisation and economic development of the region (NE) in the present era one can compare the 2nd and 3rd census report of industrialisation registered under SSI sector which can be seen from Table 2.

TABLE 2

Comparison of the Third Census with Second Census (Registered SSI Sector)

Sl. No.	*Indicator*	*2nd Census (1987-88) (Pre-globalisation)*	*3rd Census (2001-02) (Post-globalisation)*
1.	Percentage of Working Units	62.75	60.767
2.	Percentage of Working Units in rural areas	42.20	44.33
3.	Percentage of Working Units that are—		
	SSIs	96.24	65.55
	Ancillaries	0.52	5.08
	SSSBEs	3.24	34.45
4.	Percentage of proprietorship Working Units	80.48	88.85
5.	Percentage of proprietorship Working Units engaged in Manufacturing Assembly/processing	65.42	63.45
6.	Percentage of Working Units that are owned/ managed by—		
	SCs	6.84	7.85
	STs	1.70	3.53
	Women	7.69	8.32
7.	Per Working Unit Fixed Investment (Rs. lakhs)	1.60	6.68
8.	Per Working Unit Investment(original) in P&M (Rs. Lakhs)	0.95	2.21
9.	Per Working Unit production (Rs. Lakhs)	7.38	14.78
10.	Per Working Unit Employment (No.)	6.29	4.48
11.	Employment per rupee one lakh of investment in Fixed Assets	3.94	0.67
12.	Production/Employment (Rs. Lakhs)	0.04	3.30

Source: Third All India Census of Small Scale Industries, 2001-02.

The second and third all India census of small scale industries were conducted in the year 1987-88 and 2001-02 respectively which reflect the pre-globalisation and post-globalisation scenario of SSI in India. A comparison of second and third all India census of small scale industries reveals the fact that—while the proportion of working units remained the same by and large, the domination of SSI among the working units has been reduced considerably from 96 per cent to 66 per cent. This is mainly due to the increase in the number of units engaged in services, as the number of units in manufacturing sector decreases only marginally from 65.42 per cent to 63.43 per cent. The per unit employment has also come down from 6.29 to 4.48. This could be due to technological gradation and advancement being resorted to by the units in the sector in the face of the changed economic competitive conditions. As a result, the per capita fixed investment has gone up from Rs. 1.60 lakh to 6.68 lakh.

Again, SSI has been assigned as an important sector which can be witnessed as the development measures of both states and central government towards industrialisation in the said region. Table 3 shows the total SSI in NE. For the development of the NE region Government of India categorized these states as Special Category State. Under the New Industrial Policy for promoting industries in the NE states various concessions on fiscal incentives are offered as part of a package, equity contribution by the government such as; 100 per cent exemption of excise duty and income tax for ten years, capital investment subsidy of 15 per cent, interest subsidy of 3 per cent as working capital loan, etc. Even though, if one look at the data relating to the state wise distribution of distribution of industries it will be noticed that NE as a group shares a negligible amount which can be seen from Table 3.

From the evaluation of the table estimates in the 3rd census of SSI, it is that the sector comprises 3,15,847 units spreading over the length and breath of NE. Again, it is seen that the industrial scenario appears skewed in Assam among the North East States also. The NE's share in the country is 3.02 per cent.

The natures of activities of the SSI sector of NE region are shown in Table 4.

From Table 4 be can be observed that except Arunachal Pradesh and Tripura all the states of NE India have higher

TABLE 3

Total SSI Sector in NER and India

Name of the state	*No. of Registered Units*	*No. of Registered Units*	*Total*	*% in Total*
Arunachal Pradesh	25.5	997	1252	0.01
Assam	14,453	1,79,926	1,94,379	1.85
Nagaland	568	13,293	13,861	0.13
Manipur	4,599	43,400	47,999	0.46
Mizoram	2,733	8,383	11,116	0.11
Meghalaya	1,939	20,581	22,520	0.23
Sikkim	174	194	368	0.00
Tripura	959	23,393	24,352	0.23
Total of NER	25,450.5	2,90,167	315,847	3.02
Other States of India	13,45,523.5	88,56,049	102,05,343	96.98
India Total	13,74,974	91,46,216	105,21,190	100

Source: 3rd All India Census of Small Scale Industries 2001-02, Ministry of Small Scale Industries, Government of India.

TABLE 4

Distribution of Total SSI Units in NER by Nature of Activity

Name of the state	*Manufacturing Repair*	*Maintenance*	*Services*	*Total*
Arunachal Pradesh	34.53	31.71	33.7	100
Assam	41.69	27.03	31.28	100
Nagaland	74.52	11.1	14.39	100.10
Manipur	65.74	14.14	20.12	100
Mizoram	49.59	2.72	47.72	100.10
Meghalaya	59.93	17.38	22.69	100
Sikkim	63.86	2.94	33.16	100.10
Tripura	25.2	17.83	34.40	100
All India	39.69	16.36	43.95	100

Source: 3rd All India Census of Small Scale Industries, 2001-02, Ministry of Small Scale Industries, Government of India.

proportion of manufacturing units in comparison of the national figure.

Problems of Industrial Backwardness in NE

In spite of the various measures taken up by the respective state governments, central government and the others there has not been any significant improvement in the said region caused by a number of reasons which can be seen from Table 5.

Potential Areas for Industrial Development in NE

Despite of the above issues there is challenges for the development of North East Region because of endowing with:

- the natural resources, favourable agro-climatic conditions and traditionally skillful manpower available in the region,
- dense forest occupying an area of about 11,688 hectare and accounting for more than 46 per cent of the total geographical area,
- natural rubber production, NER as a whole ranks second only to Kerala in the country,
- agricultural prospects which can play an important role in industrial development by providing raw materials,
- potentiality of handloom and handicrafts
- immense reserve of gas which can generate power essential for industrial development, etc.

Roadmap for Growth of Industry in NER

The review given above on the transformation of NE states economy indicates that continuation of the process of growth demands large amounts of investible resources and their effective utilisation for solving the large scale unemployment problem (which causes insurgency and terrorism resulted in serious law and order problems in the states). The North Eastern States belonging to the Special Category States are indebted to the Planning Commission and the Government of India for their continued concern and special support.

TABLE 5

Problems of Industrial Backwardness in NE

Internal Causes		*External*
Congenial	*Otherwise*	
1. Management * Lack of Experience of promoters * Faulty planning * Locational Factor	1. Management * Inefficient/Dishonest Management * Frequent change of key personal * Poor Industrial Relations	1. Management * Industry-wide Labour unrest
2. Marketing	2. Marketing	2. Marketing * Glut-Low Price Problems * Demand Recession Domestic Global * Change in— Fashion Taste
3. Financial * Lack of Capital * Adequate Costing	3. Financial * Unplanned Fund * Faulty Costing/Price * Poor Fallow up of Sundry	3. Financial Non-availability of Finance due to (i) Credit squeeze

	Debtors * Diversion of Funds * Delayed Payment of Suppliers * Costly outside borrowings Inability to identify	(ii) Delay decision by banks (iii) Government's Action towards – a. Addl Duty b. Withdrawal of subsidy c. Restriction of import, lack of price support.
4. Production * Obsolete or inappropriate technology	4. Production * Low Productivity * Machine Breakdown * Under utilised capacity * High Wastages * High labour cost * Poor quality of raw Material * Poor machinery * Product obsolescence	4. Production * Non-availability of Raw-Materials, power, Fuel, Water, etc. * Natural Calamities.

Considering the inherent problems of NE states, the following pivot points can be taken up for implementing in the said region.

Pivot 1: Preparing a meaningful and effectuated "Look East" policy for ensuring comprehensive development of North East must be made.

Pivot 2: Development of human resources where vocational training and technology dissipation as well as entrepreneurship development are to be the key components.

Pivot 3: Improving good infrastructural facilities such as transportation, communication, electricity, etc. through upgradation is an important path.

Pivot 4: Developing the spirit of entrepreneurship must be given towards the public at large of the region.

Pivot 5: Technological innovation and skill upgradation towards more value addition in primary sector activities like agriculture, pisci-culture, and vegetable production are required.

Pivot 6: Plantation sector like tea and rubber need to be similarly given an important pivotal road.

Pivot 7: Commercial reorientation of Handloom and Handicraft sector also deserves due attention because of providing employment.

Pivot 8: Development of industries based on gas and other mineral resources can be advocated due to large reserve of the resources.

Pivot 9: Providing financial assistance using direct and indirect schemes to all the sectors is a must.

Pivot 10: Setting up the public investment in agriculture and implementing the recommendations of the National Commission for farmers must be made.

Pivot 11: Taking up the steps for fulfilling the National Common Minimum Programme (NCMP) is necessary.

Pivot 12: Taking up the Special Area Programme, namely Border Area Development Programme effectively is necessary for relocation of industries.

CONCLUSION

For the all round development of the NE economy and to fill up the gap and correct the imbalances in area development, efforts are to be made to utilise the talents of the people in industrializing and gearing up the administrative set-up. The problem of growing unemployment among the educated youth can be solved through creating more opportunities under self-employment schemes. The widening disparities among the rich and the poor and rural and urban areas should be taken care of while formulating the plan. The best way is to emphasise rural industrialisation and improvement of agricultural practices and land productivity so that the fruits of development may be shared by all. Further, there is need to check the rapid growth of population to avoid increasing pressure on land and the government in providing basic minimum amenities of life and new avenues of employment to the growing labour force. Private investment in value added productive activities should be encouraged.

REFERENCES

Anderson, Martin, and Christer Gunnarssom eds. (2003), Development and Structural Change in Asia-Pacific; Globalising Miracles or End of a Model? London: Routledge Curzon.

A.K. Agarwal, Changing Contours of Mizoram's Economy, IASSI, Vol. 12, Jan.-June, (1994), Nos. 3-4, pp. 73-81.

Gulshan Sachdeva, Preparing the Northeastern Economy for the Future, Oct.-Dec. 2005, *Eastern Quarterly*, Manipur Research Forum, Delhi.

H.C. Gautam and M.P. Bezbaruah, *Rural Transformation in North East India*, pp. 1-8, K.V. Nagaraju Credits.

India—At a glance, 2006.

Jayanti, N., Rural Poverty in NE: Problems and Prospects. *Indian Journal of Global Economy*, Forthcoming issue of November, 2006.

M. Iboton Singh, Political Economy of Manipur: Transformation within the Mixed Economy Paradigm, *Eastern Quarterly*. Vol. 3, Issue 2, Oct.-Dec., 2005.

North Eastern Council, Toward Regional Development Plans and Perspective, Publication No. 8, Jan. 1980, Shillong.

North Eastern Industrial Consultants Ltd. (1995), Report on Prospects and Possibilities of Setting up Industrial Estates in Manipur, Nagaland, Mizoram and Tripura for IDBI, Agartala.

Pratiyogita Darpan, Indian Economy (General Studies) 2006.

Planning Commission, Tenth Five Year Plan, 2002-07, Vol. 1.

Rana, Kondle and Gupta, Indian Industry in the Era of Reforms, *The Indian Journal of Commerce*, Vol. 58, No. 3, July-September 2005, pp 185-203.

Rudder Dutt and K.P.M. Sundharam, Indian Economy, 2004, S. Chand & Company Ltd.

12

Poverty, Inequality and Inclusive Growth in India

ZAFAR AHMAD SULTAN

In sum, India is now entering into a new stage of social, political, and economic development. While high GDP growth has resulted in a dramatic decrease in extreme poverty from 1990 to 2005, income and non-income inequalities are rising rapidly and, if these are not addressed, there is a major risk to continued social and economic progress in developing Asia. To address this risk, the development agenda will need to be expanded to include not only the eradication of extreme poverty, but also improving living standards of a much larger group who feel disenfranchised by the real or perceived disadvantages associated with rising inequalities in opportunities. An inclusive growth strategy will enable India not only to accomplish its mission of eradicating extreme poverty but also address the legitimate concerns of this larger segment of the population.

Three damaging developments along with the rapid economic growth seem to have been associated with India's increasing participation in the process of globalisation since the early 1990s. The first of these disquieting developments is the emergence of new kinds of inequalities as between the states of the Indian Union, and rapid widening of the old income and labour productivity gaps between states and between agriculture and other economic sectors. The second cause for concern arise from the evidence that the number of poor people in rural India increased following nearly two decades of more or less continuous improvement. The head count poverty ratios also went up in many of the states. Last but not the least, the related questions of deteriorating productive employment prospects, especially in rural areas, and the recent deindustrialisation of the Indian workforce. Such developments caused division of India into two parts. A "shining India", which is competing internationally and benefiting from the forces of globalisation, and suffering India inhabited by people who are poor and vulnerable. These two faces of India are both a beacon of hope and a symbol of despair. Merging these two faces will be the development challenge for the country in the days to come.

This paper reviews the recent evidence on these developments. Part I deals with issues of divergent regional development, rural-urban divide, and interpersonal disparity. Part II gives a brief profile of incidence of poverty in India. This is followed by an analysis of unemployment trend during the reform period in India. In final section, some of the policy measures proposed to be followed to achieve inclusive growth, which has been the main focus of the Eleventh Five Year Plan, have been discussed.

POVERTY

The pace of poverty reduction depends not only on the rate of economic growth but also how the benefits of this growth are shared, i.e., how the distribution of households' per capita income or consumption expenditure evolves. With the implementation of economic reforms since the early eighties, India experienced high rate of economic growth. Per capita GDP at 2000 constant prices increased from $317 to $588 between 1990 and 2005, growing at an annual rate of 4.2 percent, a pace that was never achieved in the past (World

Bank, 2007). This rapid growth has led to dramatic reduction in the level of extreme poverty. During the period 1983-84 to 2004-05 the share of the poor in the population at the national level came down from 45 percent to 28 percent. However, in terms of absolute numbers the decline was only marginal from 324 million to 315 millions (Planning Commission, 2006). However, this reduction in level of poverty was not uniform in all states. While all the major States experienced reduction in the percentage of the poor to varying degrees, five major States experienced increase in the number of poor during this period. These are Bihar (from 46.4 to 50.5 million), Madhya Pradesh (from 27.3 to 33.0 million), Maharashtra (from 28.5 to 31.7 million), Orissa (from 16.2 to 18.4 million) and Uttar Pradesh (from 55.2 to 63.9 million). There is also significant difference in rural and urban poverty scenario during the reform period. Gaurav Datt of World Bank (G. Datt, 1999) in his profile of poverty from 1973-74 to 1997 has shown that Head count index of poverty for the rural areas declined from 55.72 percent in 1973-74 to 35.73 percent at the annual rate of 2.7 percent. But during the reform period the rate of decline was not significantly different from zero. However, in urban areas, poverty declined continuously at the rate of 2.2 percent per annum both during pre and post-reform period. Thus, though at national level, poverty declined during the reform period, the situation in rural areas continues to worsen. Gaurav Datt identified the stagnation in rural growth as the principal cause for slowdown in the reduction of poverty.

INEQUALITIES

From 1990 to 2005, Indian development experience has been characterized by rising income and expenditure inequalities and stubbornly high levels of non-income inequalities. Using the Gini coefficient, a commonly used measure of inequality, inequality has increased during the reform period. Household expenditure surveys indicate that in India growth in per capita expenditure of the top quintile far exceeded that of the bottom quintile. The ratio of expenditure growth of the top to the bottom quintile is 3 for

India. Considering that the base year per capita mean expenditure of the bottom quintile was low to begin with compared to the top quintiles, it is clear that absolute differences in mean expenditures across quintile groups are increasing rapidly in India.

Persistent and growing inequalities in education and health attainments within countries are also a significant concern for India, and they exacerbate income inequalities (ADB, 2006). In many Asian countries, primary-school-age children from households of the poorest quintile are almost three times more likely to be out of school than those from the richest quintile. Inequalities are most prominent in health, with child mortality rates for the poorest quintile being two to three times higher than those for the richest quintiles.

Several studies in the recent past indicate that wealth and incomes have been getting concentrated in the hands of the rich in a fast globalizing world. This is true whether it is USA, UK, China or India. While corporate profits in the national incomes have been soaring, the wage share has been declining. Even within the total wages the share of the top management and high skilled professionals has been increasing at the cost of others. Most of the returns to capital are accruing to the urban rich.

According to the Asian Development Bank (ADB) study, widening differentials in earnings of the college educated *vis-à-vis* less educated individuals appear to be the single most important observable factor accounting for increasing inequality in India.

The ADB study further indicates that both relative and absolute inequality have increased in most parts of developing Asia. This picture is somewhat at odds with the earlier East Asian experience when countries like Japan, South Korea, Taiwan and Thailand experienced fast growth which was much more inclusive in nature. The reason attributed to such equitable sharing of the benefits of growth was the universal human development in terms of better education and skills as well as better health achieved by these countries before embarking on the fast growth path. The extremely non-inclusive nature of the recent economic growth in India can be attributed to the very poor human development, especially in the rural areas.

REGIONAL DISPARITIES

With the initiation of economic reforms in the early 1990s,and the decline in public investment, the private investment became the principal engine of economic development. Private investments flowed to those regions where conditions are favourable to achieve maximum return on investment. As a result states, like Maharashtra, Gujarat, Tamil Nadu, Andhra Pradesh and Karnataka, with better physical and social infrastructure, adequate forward and backward linkages and other conducive environment attracted the lion's share of private investment over the last two decades. On the other hand, States, which did not have the above characteristics, lagged behind. This differential economic performance of the last two decades has increased the regional disparities in the country. Broadly speaking, while the western and southern States have experienced faster economic growth, the northern and eastern states lagged behind. On the other hand, population growth continues to be significantly higher in the lagging regions as compared to the forward regions. As a result, the per capita income differentials have been widening even further. In a paper based on data on per capita state domestic product from 1960 to 1995, Ghosh, Marjit and Neogi (1998) find that regional disparities declined from 1961-62 to 1981-82. Since then the coefficient variation have been rising continuously, with steep increase after 1991. The per capita income of the states like Andhra Pardesh, Gujarat, Maharashtra, Haryana, Tamil Nadu increased by more than three times between 1993-94 to 2004-05, while that of other states like Bihar, Jharkand, Assam, Orissa increased by less than three percent (Economic Survey, 2006-07).

Another dimension of the same problem is that while more and more employment opportunities are created in the developed regions of the country, the labour force growth is much higher in the backward regions. This will necessarily imply that large-scale migration in search of employment will take place from the backward regions to the developed regions. This will have adverse implications socially as well as economically. Apart from the social and cultural dislocation of the migrant, the response of the recipient community also may have adverse social impact on the migrant (as is recently witnessed in Maharashtra). While the remittances of the migrant may add to the purchasing power back at home, a larger economic issue is that often migration depletes the availability of skills in the home market, which will impede the development of the region. This has also resulted in rise in farm workforce share in a growing working population.

A persistent and growing inequality in access to social services such as education and health, exacerbated by income inequalities, is also a significant concern for India. The levels of literacy and health indicators, and other social amenities have been better in the economically progressive States. They have been also known for better social cohesion and more inclusive sharing of the benefits of development (National Human Development Report and the first Social Development Report).

RURAL URBAN DIVIDE

There always existed a rural-urban divide in terms of economic and social development. But this divide has also been widening in the recent past. Ratio of urban income to rural income which was just about 1.6 in 1951 and continued to remain within reasonable limit during the first three decades of development planning to reach 2.1 in 1980-81, worsened during the last two decades to record a level close to 4.5. While large and medium cities are experiencing unprecedented economic prosperity, the rural areas have been experiencing economic stagnation. While the share of agriculture in the national income declined from about 30 per cent to almost half, the share of population dependent on agriculture remains almost the same over the last two decades. With the withdrawal of the State from critical support services for agriculture, global competition and higher risk of commercial cultivation, farmers especially those with small holdings, have been experiencing unmitigated misery. The reports of rampant farmers' suicide from various States, is only one of the symptoms of the current rural distress. A manifestation of the increasing rural distress is the growing influence of Naxalites in different parts of the country especially in the backward regions.

In sum, India is now entering into a new stage of social, political, and economic development. While high GDP growth has resulted in a dramatic decrease in extreme poverty at national level, rural poverty has increased. Further, there is constant rise in income and non-income inequalities, regional disparities, and rural-urban gap. If these are not addressed, there is a major risk to continued social and economic progress in the country.

EMPLOYMENT

Employment is an area, which shows up where our growth process is failing on inclusiveness. The number of workers is growing, particularly in non-agricultural employment, but weaknesses appear in unemployment, the quality of employment, and in large and increasing differentials in productivity and wages. Data from the latest NSS round for 2004-05, the Economic Census 2005 and the Annual Survey of Industry reveal the following:

(i) Employment growth accelerated to 2.6 per cent during 1999-2005 outpacing population growth. But the average daily status unemployment rate, which had increased from 6.1 per cent in 1993-94 to 7.3 per cent in 1999-2000, increased further to 8.3 per cent in 2004-05. This was because the working age population grew faster than total population and labour force participation rates increased, particularly among women. We are obviously not tapping the demographic dividend fully. The extent of under-employment also appears to be on the increase.

During the liberalisation period, the rate of unemployment in rural areas has increased from 5.6 percent in 1993-94 to 7.7 percent in 1999-2000, and the rate of urban unemployment marginally increased from 7.4 percent to 7.7 percent in 1999-2000 (R. Dutt, 2006).

(ii) Agricultural employment has increased at less than 1 per cent per annum, slower than population growth and much slower than growth in non-agricultural employment. This is the expected trend in long-term development but a matter of concern is that this has also been associated with a sharp increase in unemployment (from 9.5% in 1993-94 to 15.3% in 2004-05) among agricultural labour households which represent the poorest groups. Also, although real wages of these workers continue to rise, growth has decelerated strongly, almost certainly reflecting the poor performance in agriculture. There are also transition problems in changing employment patterns, and these are probably being exacerbated by our landholding structures and by barriers of caste and gender. These problems need to be addressed in the 11th Five Year Plan.

(iii) Non-agricultural employment expanded robustly at an annual rate of 4.7 per cent during 1999-2005 but this growth was entirely in the unorganized sector and mainly in low productivity self-employment. Employment in the organized sectors actually declined despite fairly healthy GDP growth. This is clearly a matter of concern since only organized sector jobs are regarded as desirable and lack of expansion in this category is a source of frustration for our increasingly educated youth who have rising expectations.

(iv) Some young workers in the knowledge economy benefit from high wage rates but NSS earnings data show negligible growth of average real wage rates in non-agricultural employment during 1999-2005. Women and less educated workers did worse than others and sizeable increases in earnings were confined mainly to those who were graduates at least. According to the Annual Survey of Industries, real wages stagnated or declined even for workers in organized industry although managerial and technical staff did secure large increase.

(v) The wage share in our organized industrial sector has halved after the 1980s and is now among the lowest in the world. One reason for this is increasing capital intensity of the organized sector, another is outsourcing. An issue for policy research is why, despite our factor endowment, organized sector has been choosing to replace labour with capital at this scale and whether there are policy distortions that encourage this which should be corrected.

The persistence of poverty, unemployment, and disparity, whether interpersonal, regional or rural-urban, could lead to three outcomes.

First, rising absolute gaps in income and consumption between the poorest and richest quintiles could trigger social and political tensions.

Second, in its extreme form, these tensions could lead to armed conflict as is currently happening in parts of India in different forms (Murshed and Gates, 2006). Rising inequalities in India pose a clear and present danger to social and political stability and, therefore, the sustainability of the growth process itself.

Third, reforms would stall, resulting in lower growth and higher inequalities.

In addressing these challenges, inclusive growth with its focus on creating economic opportunities and ensuring equal access to them will play a pivotal role. Realising this, the Government of India in its Eleventh Plan has switched to a new strategy focusing on two objectives: raising economic growth and making growth more inclusive (Planning Commission of India, 2006).

Although there is yet no widely agreed formal definition for inclusive growth, a consensus on what it entails is emerging from policy statements of various countries and their development partners, from discussions on development policies at international and regional forums, and from studies and reports of academic and policy researchers. Inclusive growth means growth with equal opportunities. Inclusive growth therefore focuses on both creating opportunities and making the opportunities accessible to all. Growth is inclusive when it allows all members of a society to participate in and contribute to the growth process on an equal basis regardless of their individual circumstances.

Inclusive growth based on equal opportunity differentiates inequalities due to individual circumstances from those due to individual efforts. An individual's circumstances such as religious background, parental education, geographical location, and caste (in India) are exogenous to and outside the control of the individual, for which he or she should not be held responsible. Inequalities due to differences in circumstances often reflect social exclusion arising from weaknesses of the existing systems of property and civil rights, and thus should be addressed through public policy interventions. On the other hand, an individual's efforts represent actions that are under the control of the individual, for which he or she should be held responsible. Inequalities due to differences in efforts reflect and reinforce market-based incentives needed to foster innovation, entrepreneurship, and growth. Incentives should not be disregarded.

The World Bank (2006) mentions two kinds of inequalities. "Inequalities of opportunities" those are mostly due to differences in individual circumstances; and "inequalities of outcome" those reflect some combination of diffences in efforts and circumstances. If policy interventions succeed in ensuring full equality of access to opportunities, inequalities in outcomes would then only reflect differences in efforts. Such inequalities according to Chaudhuri and Ravallion (2007) can be described as "good inequalities" in the sense that these are necessary to provide incentives and these are inherent for any growth process. On the other hand, if all individuals exert the same level of efforts while policy interventions cannot fully compensate for the disadvantages of circumstances, the resulting inequalities in outcomes are "bad inequalities." Equalities in opportunities, which emphasizes eliminating circumstance-related bad inequalities so as to reduce inequalities in outcomes, is at the core of inclusiveness and at the heart of an inclusive growth strategy.

Inclusive growth not only addresses the inequality

issue, but also enhances the poverty reduction agenda. First, the impact of growth on poverty reduction is higher when the initial level of inequality is lower and/or inequality declines over time. Second, inclusive growth makes poverty reduction efforts more effective by focusing on creating productive employment opportunities and making them equally accessible for all, while addressing extreme poverty through social safety nets and, therefore, moving away from the targeting approach to development. There is now a broad agreement that an effective poverty reduction strategy consists of two prongs, the first being broad-based, pro-poor economic growth based on private sector incentives to create employment opportunities; and the second being public investment in basic education, health, and infrastructure. These two prongs should be supported by social safety nets to protect the very poor and vulnerable (Kanbur, 2000).

In sum, an inclusive growth strategy encompasses the key elements of an effective poverty reduction strategy and, more importantly, expands the development agenda. A poverty reduction strategy based on a single and absolute income criterion ignores the issue of inequalities and the risks associated with them. In contrast, an inclusive growth strategy addresses circumstance-related inequalities and their attendant risks. Inclusive growth is not based on a redistributive approach to addressing inequality. Rather, it focuses on creating opportunities and ensuring equal access to them. Equality of access to opportunities will hinge on larger investments in augmenting human capacities including those of the poor, whose main asset, labor, would then be productively employed.

ELEVENTH FIVE YEAR PLAN AND INCLUSIVE GROWTH

Given that inclusive growth focuses on both creating economic opportunities and ensuring equal access to them, an effective inclusive growth strategy should have two anchors:

(i) high and sustainable growth to create productive and descent employment opportunities, and
(ii) social inclusion to ensure equal access to opportunities by all.

Eleventh Five Year Plan with an appropriately titled approach paper "Towards Faster and More Inclusive Growth" has comprehensively dealt with these two anchors. Chapter 3 titled Sectoral Policies for the Eleventh Plan describes how to accelerate the rate of growth of different sectors of the economy so that productive and descent employment opportunities can be created. The entire Chapter 4 of this Plan document deals with "Strategic Initiatives for Inclusive Development". Three areas are dealt in great details, viz. childcare, empowerment through education, and comprehensive strategy for better health. Chapter 5 "Bridging Divides: Including the Excluded" deals with the various strategies to correct the imbalances and disparities.

HIGH AND SUSTAINABLE GROWTH

For low-income country like India where the level of extreme poverty is still high, a key challenge during the next few years will be to eradicate extreme poverty by transforming their rural and agriculture-dominated economies into ones with higher agriculture productivity, and industry and services sectors playing a much greater role in terms of not only of output but also in terms of employment. This would also require continued investment in physical infrastructure and in human capital and skills; and continued efforts in improving business environment conducive to private entrepreneurships, foreign trade, and foreign investment. Chapter 3 titled Sectoral Policies for the Eleventh Plan discusses these issues in details. For example, the plan set the target of 4 per cent annual increase in growth of agriculture sector during the plan period. To fulfil the target, the emphasis were given on doubling the rate of growth of irrigated area; improvement in water management, rain water harvesting and watershed development; provision of easy access to credit at affordable rates; improvement in the incentive structure and functioning of markets; and refocus on land reforms issues.

For the promotion of industrial growth the 11th Plan set the target of raising the rate of growth of the industrial sector to 10 per cent and manufacturing growth to 12 per cent per annum. The most critical short-term barriers to growth of the manufacturing sector are absence of world-class infrastructure (power in particular), shortage of skilled manpower, inspector raj and lack of labour flexibility. The 11th Plan has placed special emphasis on infrastructure and skill formation.

SOCIAL INCLUSION

Promoting social inclusion requires public interventions in three areas: (i) investing in education, health, and other social services to expand human capacities, especially of the disadvantaged; (ii) promoting good policy and sound institutions to advance social and economic justice and level playing fields; and (iii) forming social safety nets to prevent extreme deprivation. While (i) and (ii) are essential to equalize opportunities, (iii) is needed to cater to the special needs of people who cannot participate in and benefit from the opportunities created by growth for reasons beyond their control and to alleviate transitory livelihood shocks.

(a) Expanding Human Capacities

Expanding human capacities to participate in new opportunities means investing in education, health, and other social services and other social services such as water and sanitation. Education is one of the most prominent determinants of movements out of chronic poverty. Improved health and nutrition have also been shown to have direct effects on labor productivity and individuals' earning capacities, especially among the poor. For the purpose, the 11th Plan aims at universalisation of Integerated Child Development Scheme (ICDS) that covers supplementary nutrition, immunization, monitoring of weight and height, and in some cases, crèche facilities for a limited period, to children below six years. Strong efforts also need to be made to improve accountability through greater involvement of PRIs.

The 11th Plan proposed to spend 6 percent of GDP on education. It also reiterates the fulfilment of the Constitutional obligation of providing free and compulsory elementary education of good quality to all children up to the age of 14. Besides, the plan. also focused on raising the minimum level of education to high school or Class X level, modernization of ITI and increasing in their numbers to increase the supply of trained labour to meet the growing demand for these in the market.

The 11th Plan will also address issues of sustainability by moving away wherever possible from ground water to surface water resources. Where alternate sources do not exist, or are not cost effective, ground water recharge measures will be insisted upon in the vicinity of the project.

The 11th Plan also emphasises on full and timely realisation of the Bharat Nirman targets.

(b) Good Policies and Sound Institutions

Promoting social inclusion requires good policy and sound institutions. Political, economic, cultural, and social freedoms ensure that members of a society would not be excluded from participating, contributing, and benefiting from the new economic opportunities because of their individual circumstances, or because they do not belong to certain power groups who control political and economic decision-making. Many studies have shown that along with the number of jobs created in the growth process, it is equally important to look into the quality and decency of jobs. It is now recognized that there is a strong linkage between productivity and decency of jobs. Decent jobs—which pay a fair wage rate, provide social security, offer good working conditions, and allow a voice at work—improve productivity. The 11th Plan provides an opportunity to focus on and diagnose the reasons for these failings and to reverse at least some of the adverse outcomes of the recent growth pattern. It should aim at making employment generation an integral part of the growth process and devise strategies to accelerate not only growth of employment but also of wages of the poorly paid. In order to make growth more inclusive, it is vital that more people gain access to more productive assets with which they can themselves generate decent incomes and also that GDP growth generates sufficient demand for wage labour so that those who cannot be self-employed are at least employed at decent wages. Targeting faster growth in GDP and doubling of agricultural growth will help in this process though it must be noted that this alone may not be sufficient. Further, looking at 65 million increase in labour force during the Eleventh Plan in addition to 35 million backlog of unemployed, we must plan for at least 65 million additional non-agricultural opportunities in the 11th Plan. This will not create full employment, but it will at least ensure that the unemployment rate falls somewhat. However, even this modest goal implies that the rate of growth of non-agricultural employment would need to accelerate to 5.8 per cent per annum from 4.7 per cent in 1999-2005. Furthermore, if the high unemployment among the educated youth is to be reduced and if quality of overall employment is to improve, there must be a robust growth in organized sector employment. In other words, a massive reversal is required from the negative employment growth during the last decade. Measures would need to be taken in the 11th Plan to boost, in particular, labour intensive manufacturing sectors such as food processing, leather products, footwear, and textiles, and service sectors such as tourism and construction.

(c) Social Safety Nets

Promoting social inclusion also requires the government to provide social safety nets to mitigate the effects of external and transitory livelihood shocks as well as to meet the minimum needs of the chronically poor. Such shocks are often created by ill-health, macroeconomic crises, industrial restructuring, and natural disasters. Social safety nets serve two main purposes. First, by providing a floor for consumption, they are a coping mechanism for the very poor and the unfortunate. Second, they could provide insurance against risk to enable vulnerable people to invest in potentially high-return activities to lift themselves up by their bootstraps, i.e., social safety nets serve as springboards to enable vulnerable people to break out of poverty (World Bank, 2001). By encouraging efforts, safety nets could contribute toward greater equality in outcomes.

Social safety nets typically take the following forms: (i) labor market policies and programs aimed to reduce risks of unemployment, underemployment, or low wages resulting from inappropriate skills or poorly functioning labor markets; (ii) social insurance programs designed to cushion risks associated with unemployment, ill health, disability, work-related injuries, and old age, examples being pensions, health and disability insurance, and unemployment insurance; (iii) social assistance and welfare schemes such as welfare and social services, and cash or in-kind transfers intended for the most vulnerable groups with no other means of adequate support, such as single-parent households, victims of natural disasters or civil conflicts, handicapped people, or the destitute poor; and (iv) child protection to ensure the healthy and productive development of children, examples being early child development programs, school feeding programs, scholarships, free or subsidized health services for mothers and children, and family allowances or credit.

Currently, one of the programmes which provides safety nets to the unorganized sector workers is National Social Assistance Programme This programme has two components: the National Family Benefits Scheme that provides a lump sum benefit of Rs 10,000 in the case of death of the primary breadwinner in a BPL family; and the National Old Age Pensions Scheme which provides pension at the rate Rs 200 per month to aged destitute persons with little or no regular means of subsistence. This is virtually the only social security available to unorganized sector workers, although some states do provide additional packages for specified workers.

There are some other programmes and policies that also constitute elements of a social safety net against vulnerabilities, such as the targeted public distribution system, the Indira Awaas Yojana, National Rural Health Mission and various types of crop and livestock insurance. We do not, however, yet have a comprehensive social safety net covering the bulk of our population, particularly people in the informal sector. Without this, we do not have a comprehensive strategy for tackling poverty. The 11th Plan proposed to increase the scope for expanding and reshaping existing schemes and adding new schemes to improve the social safety net needs to be carefully examined.

One of the criticism of our labour legislation is that it has singularly failed to give any protection or security in terms of working conditions or wages to about 93 per cent of the total workers who work in the unorganized sectors, including agriculture. Extending labour protection to the unorganized sector is obviously difficult to implement but the time has come during the 11th Plan to evolve policy initiatives which makes a beginning by offering a modicum of protection and security to the unorganized sector workers, with respect to working conditions, wages, medical insurance facilities and some sort of pension benefits through the joint efforts of the central and state governments, as well as the employers and workers themselves. The Second National Commission of Labour had made some recommendations pursuit to its remit to propose umbrella legislation to ensure at least minimum protection and welfare for unorganized sector workers. Subsequently, the National Commission for Enterprises in the Unorganized Sector has drawn up the draft legislation, along with a scheme for social protection, which is under consideration. One way to proceed expeditiously would be to enact a legislation that provides core benefits to the poorest and commits to progressive enlargement of benefits and extension of coverage.

RURAL URBAN DIVIDE

The 11th Plan proposes to take action on both fronts. The strategy of accelerated agricultural development combined with infrastructure support for non-agricultural activity in rural areas, will help reduce the urban-rural divide. Programme such as Bharat Nirman are particularly relevant in this context.

CONCLUSION

The above discussion reveals that in India during the reform period, though there was rapid increase in growth of the economy, the cake of this growth has not been shared equally by all segments of the society. Various dimensions of economic and social disparity- regional, rural-urban, social class or gender have aggravated in the recent period. The number of poor people in rural India increased following nearly two decades of more or less continuous improvement. The head-count poverty ratios also went up in many of the states. There is rise in unemployment in urban as well as in rural areas both, due to decline in absorptive capacity of agriculture and sharp decline in output elasticity of employment in organized sector.

The evidence suggests that what the situation now requires is the adaptation and strengthening of certain existing procedures and institutions and establishing of atleast one new one. Realising this, the government in the Eleventh Five Year Plan has now shifted its development strategy from poverty reduction and redistribution strategy to inclusive growth strategy, which consists of two strategic pillars, namely, (i) Investing in Creating Opportunities to support high and sustainable growth in DMCs; and (ii) Investing in Broadening Access to Opportunities to support social inclusion in developing Asia. If the things go well in the desired direction as is conceived in the plan, may, to some extent, lessen some of these disturbing outcomes of the reform period.

References

Asian Development Bank (2006), *Key Indicators*, Asian Development Bank, Manila.

Chaudhuri, S., and M. Ravallion (2007), "Partially Awakened Giants Uncover Growth in China and India." In L. Alan Winters and S. Yusuf, (eds.), *Dancing with Giants: China, India, and the Global Economy*, The World Bank, Washington, DC.

Council for Social Development (2006), *India—Social Development Report*, New Delhi: Oxford University Press.

Datt, Gaurav (1999), "Has Poverty Declined since Economic Reforms", *Economic and Political Weekly*, Vol. XXXIV, No. 50, pp. 11-17.

Datt, Gaurav and Ravillion, M. (2002), "Is India's Economic Growth Leaving the Poor Behind", *Journal of Economic Perspectives*, Vol. 16, No. 3.

Datt, Rudar (2001), Economic Liberalisation and Its Implications for Employment in India", *Indian Economic Association 84th Conference Volume*, pp. 461-89.

Ghosh, B., Marjit, S. and Neogi, N. (1998), "Economic Growth and Regional Divergence in India, 1960-95", *Economic and Political Weekly*, Vol. XXXIII, No. 26, pp. 1623-30.

Government of India, *Economic Survey*, New Delhi, Various issues.

Government of India (2002), *National Human Development Report, 2001*, Planning Commission, New Delhi.

Kanbur, R. (2000), "Income Distribution and Development". In A.B. Atkinson and F. Bourguignon, eds., *Handbook of Income Distribution*, Amsterdam, North-Holland.

Murshed, S.H., and S. Gates (2006), "Spatial-Horizontal Inequality and the Maoist Insurgency in Nepal." *Review of Development Economics*, Vol. 9, No. 1, pp. 121-34.

Planning Commission (2006), *Approach Paper to Eleventh Five Year Plan*, Government of India, Yojana Bhavan, New Delhi.

World Bank, 2001, *From Safety Net to Springboard*, Washington, DC., World Bank, 2006, "Equity and Development", In *World Development Report, 2006*, Washington, DC.

World Bank (2006), "Equity and Development", *World Development Report, 2006*, Washington, DC.

World Bank (2007), *World Development Indicators*, Washington, DC.

13

Economic Development: Problems and Prospects of Weaker Section of Society in Bihar

BHARAT BHUSHAN, SHEKHER AND KABITA KUMARI

Bihar is the heart of the Indian economy. No one can expect development of India without economic development of Bihar. Bihar is the third largest populous state of India after U.P. and Maharashtra, having 82,878,796 population according to the 2001 census of India. Bulk of the Bihari's population lives in condition of misery. Poverty is not only acute but also chronic in Bihar. At the same time there exits unutilised land of north Bihar due to flood situation. The co -existence of vicious circle of poverty with the vicious circle of affluence perpetual misery and foils all attempts at removal of poverty.

Basically economic development implies the process of securing level of productivity in all sectors of economy and this is turn, is a function of the level of technology for obtaining a higher level of technology, the Bihar economy is required to forge the physical apparatus in the form of machines, equipments, tools and instruments of productions on the one hand and on the other, to train the labor force of the state of Bihar and India to make use of physical apparatus thus created. In a nut shell, econom ic development is a process of stepping up the rate of capital formation. But it must be emphasized the capital, through necessaries is not a sufficient condition of economic development which depends on such as non-economic factors as social attitudes, Political conditions, human endowments and efficient governance. Economic developments thus depends on two sets of factors: Economic factors, and Non economic factors.

STATUS OF WEAKER SECTION OF SOCIETY

"Necessitous men are not free man" said Frenklyn Roosevelt in 1941. It is true to its words. A large number of people belonging to weaker section of society especially scs&sts in Bihar are living in abject poverty. As per the 2001 census of India there are 13.7 crore rural families in the country living below the poverty line. About 4.5 crore people only in Bihar living below the poverty line. They are the real necessitous men. These starta of the population are leading a life of economic insecurity.

Economic security matters become human freedom and dignity matters to every human beings. Real freedom cannot exist unless a certain level of economic security is achived. Economic security is linked with labour market security, income security, job security, is profection against loss of income earning work, or it refers to the sense of attachment to a current enterprise, job security refers to the sense of attachment to a particular job. Work security is about working conditions that are safe and promote workers well-being. A good society is one that guarantees all its members' equal basic economic security. This required at least a minimal income to the weaker section on which to survive in decency in society.

At present very few Industrial manufacturing units were in the state therefore the share of workers employed in non-agricultural activities to the work force, is below 19 per cent the number of total workers to total population of Bihar is 33.38 per cent.

TABLE 1

Trends in Rural Non-farm Employment in Bihar

Census Year	*Percentage of RNFE*
1961	19.77
1971	15.31
1981	18.22
1991	18.90
2001	18.78

The table above shows the declining trend over the decades.

TABLE 2

Sector-wise Trends of Work Force in Bihar

Census Year	*Agricultural Sector*	*Non-agricultural Sector*
1961	80.23	19.77
1971	84.69	15.31
1981	81.18	18.22
1991	81.10	18.90
2001	81.22	18.78

The above table shows that in case of non-form employment in Bihar, there is no significant increase in percentage observed during the five decades.

Due to employment of majority population of Bihar in the Agricultural sector where the per capita income is very low the percentage belonging to below poverty line is very high in the state of Bihar.

Among the states in terms of percentage Orissa has the Dubious distinction of having the highest proportion 47.15 per cent of its population living the below poverty line. It is followed by Bihar which has 42.60 per cent of its population categorized as poor during the year 1999-00.

But in terms of Sheer number it is U.P. with tops the list with around 5.3 crore people below the poverty live. Bihar with about 4.5 crore of the people occupies second place in the year 1999-2000.

THE CAUSES OF MARGINALISED PEOPLE FOR NOT GETTING THE BENEFITS OF ECONOMIC DEVELOPMENT

From the above that there is no denying the facts that process if socio-economic transformation leading to over all development has already started in our country along with states. At the same time there should not any denying of the fact that the process has been too slow and there is disturbing deceleration in the process of development accompanied by hightened disparities as a whole range of indictors that signal the nature of development.

Despite spending huge money on different five year plans and all the provisions enshrined in the Indian constitution, there lot has not improved completely. We can not deny changing the condition of marginalised people of different society but hope of the complete diminution of their poverty and paucity remains defeated.

In my view the condition that prevails among the weaker section of the society does not benefited due to lack of major issues of development.

In my opinion there are the main issues due to which the benefits of grouth does not reach. The poorer section of the population, especially unorganized workers, dalits and other marginalised section of Bihar. These are:

(i) Lack of awareness due to lack of education among weaker section of the society.
(ii) Low per capita income and low rate of economic growth.
(iii) Vicious circle of poverty among weaker section people of Bihar.
(iv) Low level of productive efficiency due to in inadequate nutrition and malnutrition.
(v) Malpractices in every department.
(vi) Imbalances between population size, resources and capital.
(vii) Problems of unemployment specially among weaker section people due to lack of industrialisation.
(viii) Imbalances between agricultural wages and non-

TABLE 3

Precentage of RNPF and Urbanisation in Bihar (2001 Census)

Sl. No.	District	% of RNPF	% of Urbansation
1.	Agra	4.88	6.24
2.	Aurangabad	8.46	8.42
3.	Banka	7.33	7.13
4.	Begusarai	11.17	4.58
5.	Bhagalpur	13.89	18.95
6.	Bhojpur	8.77	13.98
7.	Buxor	9.29	9.18
8.	Champaran East	5.64	8.74
9.	Champaran West	5.69	6.39
10.	Darbbanga	9.04	8.12
11.	Gaya	9.24	13.71
12.	-Gopalganj	6.79	6.07
13.	Jahanabad	7.65	7.40
14.	Jammui	7.12	7.38
15.	Kaimur	17.15	3.23
16.	Katihar	6.82	9.13
17.	Khagariya	7.78	5.97
18.	Kisanjanj	7.05	3.84
19.	Lakhisarai	7.67	14.68
20.	Madhepura	4.14	4.46
21.	Madubani	6.24	5.74
22.	Munger	17.15	27.88
23.	Muzaffarpur	9.72	9.30
24.	Nalanda	9.94	14.92
25.	Nawada	7.82	7.66
26.	Patna	20.36	41.80\
27.	Purnea	5.93	9.47
28.	Rohatash	9.30	13.39
29.	Saharsa	5.04	08.23
30.	Samastipur	7.76	03.62
31.	Saran	7.02	9.17
32.	Shekhpura	10.27	15.48
33.	Shibahar	9.97	4.15
34.	Sitamarhi	5.90	10.17
35.	Siwan	6.98	05.45
36.	Supaul	8.81	05.04
37.	Vaishali	8.22	6.88

The above table shows the variation in Percentage of RNFE in most of the Cases due to level of urbanisation of the Districts. The data per cent of RNFE varies from 4.86 per cent in Madhepura to 23.36 per cent in Patna. Simultaneously the same trend for the per cent of urbanisation has been of turned in the above districts.

agricultural wages and also between male and female.

(ix) Instability of output of agriculture and related sections.

(x) Imbalances in distribution and growing inequalities.

(xi) Less expenditure on agriculture of GDP.

(xii) Insecurity in agricultural sectors.

SUGGESTIVE MEASURES

We have passed 57 years of planned development efforts but Bihar finds it rest in the grip of the vicious circle of poverty poor health poor education unemployment, inequbility. Shortage of wage goods, poor political economy, Lack of political will and poor development of rural area. In fact the State of Bihar has a strikingly low base of development and today it is at the bottom judged from all accepted indicatory of development, poverty, no availability of work and lower wages compel poor people to migrate to other places. 1991 census report that about 40 Lakh people migrated in metropolitan cities of India, Tea States in Assam and agricultural forms in Punjab and Haryana.

If the estimates of the course of poverty during the last decade are an accurate reflection of the development on the Ground, it would call for a re-orientation and correction of policies in a number of a areas. Board-based and labour-intensive growth is essential for a substantial reduction of poverty. A transformation of agriculture must be central to such a growth process in Bihar. For this purpose direct targeting of poor is needed of the hour. It implies that if the poor can be identified on a household or individual level transfer payment and or some other form of direct assistance can reduce their vulnerability to adjustment. It providing assistance directly to the vulnerable poor is not feasible then intervening on the basics of the characteristics of the poor may be required such as food and wage subsidies.

Successful intervention to reduce the impact of structural adjustment must be based on some mechanism for targeting assistance by way of basic needs to the poor. For this we need to use mechanism which leakage while being administratively simple for this purpose.

(i) We need a consolidiation of many anti-poverty agencies, every state government already has, to eliminate duplication of work and thus generate a surplus to handle the new schemes.
(ii) More than 70% scheduled castes and scheduled tribes are poor. So targeting these groups automatically reduces leakages.
(iii) The really backward, poor district is well known, so targeting schemes at these districts will reduce leakages. For example, in North Bihar government should started flood control measures.
(iv) Studies suggest that nearly 15% of IRDP beneficiaries have risen above the poverty line. So such beneficiaries constitute a body of the pre-identified persons.
(v) At protect reservation is not a real solution for uplifting the condition of weaker section people because creamy layer reaps the whole benefits of reservation. So I am of the clear view that creamy layer should be out of the preview of reservation policies.
(vi) Reservation policies should be based on economic status irrespective of caste.
(vii) Immediate arrangements should be made to ensure free education not only primary and secondary but also higher and technical education for all poorer people of the society who are on the border line of marginalisation.
(viii) Government should provide loans to poorer people at minimum rate of interest for their development.
(ix) Whatever laws, enactments or other measures are adoptable which affect the lives of the poorer people of state these should be given full publicity promptly from door to door and village to village thereby to inform the poorer people of society of their rights.

(x) The government of Bihar should judge result not by statistics or the amount of money spent but by the quality of human character that is involved.

(xi) Education should be compulsory and liberal to stam out illiteracy and improved the condition of depressed class of Bihar.

(xii) In sum, while targeting is too costly to be worth while improved targeting can be done cheaply and with a minimum of hassels.

It is matter of great pleasure for the poorer, marginalised and weaker section of the society, especially Dalit and minority of Bihar that the present progressive C.M. of Bihar Mr. Nitish Kumar is very promt to abolish the poverty from Bihar and make Bihar a developed state of India that is why the Vikas Porush of Bihar Shri Nitish Kumar who has the high political will is implementing various programs for the upliftment of weaker section of the society and for the empowerment of women in the state .

The present Bihar government declares 2008 the agricultural year for the development of agricultural sector by which the government wants to uplift 70% of weaker section who are fully dependent on agriculture for their livelihood.

The present government of Bihar has implemented various programs for example:

1. The government has constituted a maha dalit commission for the upliftment of four downtrodden castes of Bihar who are actually at the bottom till now.
2. The government has implemented a Kanya Bibah Yojna for the poorer people whose annual income is Rs. 60000, will get Rs. 5000. This Yojna was inaugurated by her excellency Mrs. Prtibha Devi Singh Patil, Honourable President of India on 16th Feburuay 2008 at Patna.
3. The government has implemented a Yojna in which Rs. 700 is paying for the dress of school going girls for 1 year.
4. The government of Bihar is providing bicycle for

girl students of ninth and tenth classes belonging to rural area of Bihar.

5. The government of Bihar is going to provide free coaching facilites and scholarship for those Muslim students who will stood first division at matriculation examination.
6. The Bihar government is alone in India which has implemented Kissan Samman Yojna, Kissan Ratna Yojna and Kissan Shri Yojana for the upliftment of agricultural sector of Bihar.
7. Bihar is also the first state of India which provides 50 per cent reservation for women in the panchayti raj system for the upliftment and pariciption in policies making for the development of Bihar.
8. Bihar government is also implementing Assa Yojna for the weaker section women belonging to rular and urban areas of the state of Bihar.
9. The government of Bihar has arranged a Kissan Panchayat on 17.02.08 at Patna for the upliftment of agriculturists in which 2000 agriculturist had participated from different parts of the state of Bihar.

14

Inclusive Inequality and Indian Farmer

DR. DAYANIDHI PRASAD ROY

INTRODUCTION:

The Indian economy seems set to record a near 9 percent growth for the fourth straight year now. There are many features of the economy that would seem to be quite upbeat. The saving and environment rates have now recorded unprecedented levels of ground 34 present of GDP. These alone give hope for a sustained growth rate of upwards of 8 percentage points on a crude Harrods Dommar formulation if the capital-output ratio is assumed to be around 4. Tax revenue collections seems to be booming. The foreign exchange reserves are at their most comfortable level ever. Business and industry seems to be optimistic and the stock market in the past year has had a series of sustained rallies. The percentage of the absolute poor continues to be same where around 28% of the population. But it is also relevant to consider that there is a significant fraction of the population that is technically above the poverty lines but is virtually at the margins of subsistence. Using this some what wider notions the National Commission for enterprises in the unorganized sector estimates that the percentage of population that may be regarded as being 'vulnerable' is around 77 per cent of populations.[1]

Indian economy has failed to transform the lives of the majority. The first study on informal an unorganized employment in India complied by the government mandated National Commission for Enterprises in the Unorganised Sector (NCEUS) reveals that a staggering 394.9 million or 86 per cent of the country's total work force toil in this sector without any social security net and nearly 80 per cent of these worker's live on less than Rs. 20 per day or Rs. 600 per month. These people as the panels chairman Arjun Sen Gupta rightly says are the "real poor and vulnerable" with few livelihood options and this category consists of Scheduled Tribes, Scheduled Castes. Other Backward classes and Muslims. The report adds that while the number of those who are below the official poverty line have come down in recent decades, the number of those in this broader segment of poor and vulnerable have steadily gone up.

In a sense the inequality story or the phenomenon of lack of inclusive growth in India is similar to that witnessed through the last century across the US and Europe. (That said despite high-growth income, inequality is lower than in China as the recent Asian Development Bank study has shown.) In his hypothesis, Simon Kuznet, the pioneer of research on inequality, says economic inequality increases over time till the economy attains a critical income before it begins to fall. This is because in the first stage of economy development, physical capital is the main driver of growth. In a more mature economy, human capital takes the pace of physical takes the place of physical capital as the main source of growth slowing down inequality.[2]

The results of the do not argue well for a nation that is keen to shed its developing country tag. It also shows that our service sector-driven economic growth is not broad-based and has not created employment opportunities for the marginalised.[3]

SECTORAL INEQUALITY

One of the most significant conundrums of the development process is the past decade and a half has been an apparent duality where the top fifth of the population seems to have made good in a substantial way whereas the bottom four-fifth have been more or less bypassed. Stories of suicide deaths by formers from Andhra Pradesh to Maharashtra and even Punjab are routinely reported is news papers. While the salaries of corporate bounce in metropolises are reaching dizzying heights the mass of unskilled laboures from the country side can only aspire to jobs as factory workers or security guards in the urban informal sector as pittance wages. These are wages at the bare margins of survival. These are calibrated by employers across the country to insurance that a potential worker is given just the barest minimum wage and no more. The demographic pressure from countryside is so huge that there is indeed an unlimited supply of labour at the subsistence wage as was theorized by W. Arther Lewis and earlier emphasized by classical writers like Ricardo and Marx.[4]

The numbers of poor are shocking. At 301 million, a fourth of the population (of 1,111 million) is living of less than a dollar a day. Below the low tide of poverty otherwise jargonized as BPL. Within South Asia, India has 77 per cent of the poor.

India is also home to 36 dollar-billionaires. At the height to the stock market boom, the wealth of just five individuals in the country exceeded $ 100 per cent of the GDP.

You could argue that much of this is anecdotal evidence and that poverty has come down in the post-liberalisation era. Indeed, there is clear evidence of a trickle-down effects. Poverty level has dropped by 8.38 per cent, in the 10-year period between 1993-94 and 2004-05. Yes, there is growth and the poor are earning more but the distance between the poor and the rich, whether in farms of in the metros, is widening.[5]

Study (based on data from National Sample Survey Organisation—(NSSO)—1993-94 and 2004-05 reports on expenditure and income shows that barring Jammu and Kashmir, inequality as measured by the Gini coefficient has gone up across the country. Inequality indeed, is the only constant across states, castes, religions and segments. The phenomenon is best illustrated by one critical piece of statistic. Among wage and salary earners, the top 20 per cent of the population in urban India earns 56 per cent of the income whole the bottom 20 per cent barely 3.4 per cent of the income. Indeed the top 20 per cent earns more than all the other put together. Interestingly, the rate of income growth for the middle class among salary and wage earners (see middle class squeeze) is the lowest.[6]

The state specific percentage and number of poor estimated URP consumption distribution is given in Table 1 below:

TABLE I

S. No.	States/U.Ts	Combined		S. No.	States/U.Ts	Combined	
		%age of Persons	No. of Persons (Lakhs)			%age of Persons	No. of Persons (Lakhs)
1.	Andhra Pradesh	15.8	126.10	19.	Mizoram	12.6	1.18
2.	Arunachal Pradesh	17.6	2.03	20.	Nagaland	19.0	3.99
3.	Assam	19.7	55.77	21.	Orissa	46.4	178.49
4.	Bihar	41.4	369.15	22.	Punjab	8.4	1.63
5.	Chhattisgarh	40.9	90.96	23.	Rajasthan	22.1	134.89
6.	Delhi	14.7	22.93	24.	Sikkim	20.1	1.14
7.	Goa	13.8	2.01	25.	Tamil Nadu	22.5	145.62
8.	Gujarat	16.8	90.69	26.	Tripura	18.9	6.38
9.	Haryana	14.0	32.10	27.	Uttar Pradesh	32.8	590.03
10.	Himachal Pradesh	10.0	6.36	28.	Uttarakhand	39.6	35.96
11.	Jammy and Kashmir	5.4	5.85	29.	West Bengal	24.7	208.36
12.	Jharkhnad	40.3	116.39	30.	A and N Islands	22.6	0.92
13.	Karnataka	25.0	138.89	31.	Chadigarh	7.1	0.74
14.	Kerala	15.0	49.60	32.	Dadra & N. Hav.	33.2	0.84
15.	Madhya Pradesh	38.3	249.68	33.	Daman and Diu	10.5	0.21
16.	Maharashtra	30.7	317.38	34.	Lakshadweep	16.0	0.11
17.	Manipur	17.3	3.95	35.	Pondicherry	22.4	2.37
18.	Meghalaya	18.5	4.52				

Source: Kurukshetra, May 2007, p. 45.

More important this would have gone in a large way to arrest the widening of the hiatus between the shining and 'suffering' India. While 36 Indian US dollar billionaires have assets equal to 25 per cent of our GDP, 78 per cent of Indian people live on less than Rs. 20 a day. Alas the opportunity to improve the level of livelihood of the vast majority of our people has been wasted.

Whatever the gain of liberalisation, they have not been passed on the poor and struggling farmer. The new prosperity has remained a largely urban phenomenon, entirely excluding those on the margins of our society.

As the most vulnerable section, Dalits are among those worst affected by the reforms regime. Dwindling job opportunities in public sector units owing to the government's rigorous pursuit of the policy of liberalisation and privatization have made a mockery of reservation. With little possibility of extending reservation to the private sector, they are threatned with growing unemployment. The neglect of agriculture has already caused enormous difficulties to the marginal landholders and agricultural workers, a considerable number of whom are Dalits. Loss of jobs and cuts in wages stare them in the face.

If one were to look at the comparison of the population that is vulnerable them, one finds them it is predominantly comprised those belongs to the SCs and STs, the minorities and the OBCs. They are typically individuals with low or negligible assets and with minimal education. The real issue is therefore, whether this growth of economy making exercise can bring about any difference to this huge segment of the population.

In terms of output growth rate, it is the service sector which has witnessed the highest growth rate across all sectors while agriculture is still hovering below 4 per cent mark and secondary sector growth rate (comprising of manufacturing and industry) has not gone up more than 8 per cent. In order to generate more employment, these two sectors are vital and secondary sector has to grow at around 10 per cent or so both from the point of view of generating more GDP growth and employment growth.[7]

The first authoritative study on the state of informal or unorganized employment in India complied by National Commission for Enterprises in the unorganized sector (NCEUS) a government-affiliated body reveals, which shows the employment situation in Table 2.

TABLE 2

Distribution of Main Workers by Different Industrial Categories, India 2001

Industrial category	*Main Workers*	*Percentage*
Total Main Workers*	312,972	100.0
Agricultural and allied activities	176,979	56.6
Mining and quarrying	1,908	0.6
Manufacturing	41,848	13.4
Electricity, gas and water supply	1,546	0.5
Construction	11,583	3.7
Wholesale, retail trade and repair work, Hotel and restaurants	29,333	9.4
Transport, storage and communication	12,535	4.0
Financial intermediation, real estate, business activities	6,109	2.0
Other services	31,131	10.0

Note: * Total main workers is based on actual values of Cultivators and Agricultural Laborers from full count (included in Agricultural and allied activities) and estimated values for industrial categories.

Source: India today September 24, 2007, p. 43.

Indian illustrates best the impact of globalisation on income distribution. While wages for English-speaking graduates are rising fast as information technology sector thrives, salaries for unskilled laborers are stagnating.

The second important factor is physical infrastructure. Consider the road connectivity figures. States like Madhya Pradesh and Chhattisgarh have barley 15 per cent road connectivity. This leads to income disparity between those in rural areas. Lack of connectivity from, say fields to markets, prevents farmers from getting better returns. Lack of farm-to-fork chain systems results in produce being wasted. This widens the distance between income earned from the real potential.

The latest NSSO survey reveals that average per capital expenditure of people living in urban areas is Rs. 1.052 against Rs. 558.78 in rural areas.

The wide disparity in literacy levels across states, say Bihar which has a literacy level of 46 per cent and Mizoram of 89 per cent, illustrates this best. To gauge the impact of education. Juxtapose the levels of literacy with the per capita income of the two states. Bihar has a per capita income of Rs. 6,311 while Mizoram boasts of a per capita income of Rs. 27,733. Chandigarh to have the highest per capita income in the country at Rs. 70.662.

In the most populous states, less than 50 per cent of children over the age of 10 have completed primary education. Primary health and infant mortality rates are again highest in the most populous states. Any health emergency in a low-income family can instantly push it below the poverty line.

Government not reforms the labour laws enabling those living off less than Rs. 20 a day to gain better incomes and promote the concept of doles to the unorganized sector?[8]

FARM SECTOR DISTRESS

Agriculture in contrast, has barely managed a growth rate of around 2.5 percentage points. The share of agriculture as a fraction of GDP in consequence has secularly declined from about 60 per cent at the time of independence to about 60 per cent at the time of independence to about 19 per cent now. But the share of the population dependent on the rural sector continues to be as high as about two-thirds. This has resulted insignificant is on immiserisation of farm sector in per capita term *vis-a-vis* industry and service. There has been a significant increase a rural landlessness in recent years which has direct consequences on the issue of poverty. The single major deficiency in the recent Indian growth process is its poor showing on the employment generation front for those in the countryside who are landless and without any other asset other than their labour power. The only means of redressing poverty would be to offer them employment.[9]

After all, how can we claim to be an emerging superpower when our farmers continue to kill themselves from depression and despair ? Farmers in his stall were drinking pesticide and killing themselves (and often their families) because they saw no points in living and no hope for the future.

In 1993-94, 9.5 percent of our rural population was unemployed. In 2004-05 that figure went up to 15.3 percent. So, far from creating wealth for farmers, the so-called new prosperity has actually left them unemployed. Inevitably, they have survived by borrowing. An astonishing 48.6 percent of farm house holds are in debt. And of that figure, 61 percent consists of poor farmers with holding below one hectare.[10] How hard it to see that a situation where four of the world's 10 richest people are Indians and yet lakhs of farmers kill themselves in entirely unacceptable in any fair and civilised society.

The heart of the problem lies in the fact that the costs of cultivation have risen phenomenally since the reform process began in 1991. He estimates that the per acre cost of cultivation has gone up from Rs. 2,500 in 1991 to Rs. 13,500 today.[11] It is this disconnect between the cost of cultivation and prices for the produce that is pushing increasing number of our farmer into life crushing indebtedness.

If people do not earn how will they spend or sauce Agriculture, the report found was a fertile ground for poverty, especially for small and marginal farmers, 84 per cent of whom spend more than they earned and were often caught in debt traps.

What can Rs. 20 possibly fetch? For 836 million Indian, Rs. 20 per day or Rs. 600 a month essentially buys them their daily sustenance. Technically a large chunk of these 836 million Indians—77 per cent of countries population—are above the poverty line at Rs. 12 per day. Table 3 shows agrarian crisis.

In terms of the human development index India occupies the 128th place in a listing of some 177 countries and any serious redressed of this must address the question of social sector spending for the common masses in a much more substantial way than we have done so far. Debt-stricken

TABLE 3

Low Income Levels in Rural Areas Reflect the Agrarian Crisis

Sectors	*50th Employment Round (1993-94)*	*61st employment Round (2004-05)*	*Growth annualised*
RURAL	Rs. 17,172	Rs. 47,767	9.7 %
URBAN	Rs. 44, 802	Rs. 134,113	10.5 %
NATIONAL	Rs. 24,981	Rs. 73,145	10.3 %

Source: India Today, September 24, 2007, p. 43.

farmers in Andhra Pradesh, Karnataka, Maharashtra and Punjab have resorted to suicides in the past few years. While the causes, details and impulses for these may vary it is clear that indebted farmers, apart from needing a better crop insurance regime and adequate infrastructure are certainly entitled to some relief.

Trends indicate that agricultural productivity will decline up to 25 per cent. In some countries decline in yield in rain fed agriculture could be as much as 50 per cent, crop failure distress scale of livestock and livelihood insecurity are some of the factors in which climate change will affect small farmers.[12] A permanent solution to this problem is possible by reaching privileges of development to the lower strata of people through land reform, one measure not only extremism will be controlled but substantive increase in production of food grains will also be realised.

By expanding sugar industry and re-opening the closed sugar factories again the government would send a massage to farmers for sound rural economy; this would mean a revolutionary change in rural life. Along with sector like power agro-industries and irrigation project there is a vast scope for developing the education and health sectors. Compatibility and harmony can be maintained both in human resources and economic development. It is clear from the data given in Table 4, that large chunk of agricultural labour migrate for job.

Minimum support price (MPS) for the produce is ensured "indebtedness among the farmer's cannot be prevented. The commission of Agricultural cost and prices has recommended that 24 agricultural products must be given MSP, yet, the government keeps talking of MSP for rice and wheat only. Under service pressure, from those who have pointed out that the government is importing wheat at prices substantially higher than MSP of Rs. 850 per quintal for domestic farmers, this has now been increased to Rs. 1,000. A similar increase for paddy being universally demanded has not yet been announced. However, unless all these 24 agricultural products are brought under the net of MSP, the pressures on the formers to slide back into indebtedness can not be prevented.[13]

TABLE 4

Reasons for Out-Migration from the Villages

Reasons	*Agricultural Labour*	*Other Rural Labour*
Not Sufficient work in the villages	60	34
Skilled work only outside village	11	16
Expectation higher income	8	17
Group Affinity	20	31
Social factors		12
Indebtedness	51	40
All	150	150

Source: *India Today*, September 24, 2007, p. 43.

SUGGESTION

There are clearly the major imperatives that any serious economic intervention ought really to address. The first is to channelise massive resource into the agriculture sector so as to substantially enhance productivity in this sector. This has to be done by strengthening rural infrastructure especially irrigation. The high growth rate of the Indian economy has been largely filled by the services and industry sectors that have grown at 10 or more percentage points.

In fact of the matter is that Indian agriculture is doing badly and those whose livelihood depends on it are suffering. A programme like the rural employment guarantee programme is useful only as a welfare program. It cannot really do much to overall national employment. For that we have to create conditions which enables and encourage the private sector to employ more workers. The way to tackle the problem is to step up on agricultural investment in a very big way to boost manufacturing so that more people move out of agriculture to the industrial sector.

On irrigation, minor irrigation, co-operative, Animal Husbandry and even Road construction will also benefit the farm sector.

Hence, both for the sake of Indias food security and overall economic development, it is necessary to sharply increase public investment in agriculture. Increase in public investments is the pre-condition to realize existing potential in our agricultural sector M.S. Swaminathan informs us that the prevailing gap between potential and actual yields in the crops of rain-fed areas such as Jowar, Bajra, Millets, Pulses is over 200 percent even with the technologies on the shelf. Thus while the loan waiver will provide immediate relief to the farmer they must be supported by higher investments and a structure of synergetic packages.

While there has been an 18 per cent increase in the revenues, the capital expenditures are slated to grow by less than 9 per cent instead of using these surpluses for higher public investments they have been used to reduce the deficits. Such a preoccupation with fiscal fundamentalism in an environment of high revenue buoyancy is not good economics.

Considering that the majority of the unorganised sector work force is in the agriculture sector and this sector has its own distinct problems it is important that their needs are seen separately from others. The 13 point action programme charted out by the NCEUS which includes a national security scheme, minimum conditions of work, special programme for marginal and small farmers, credit for farmers and universalisation of the National Rural Employment Guarantee Programme and the removal of the 100 day cap among others must be adhered to if the government wants to keep its promises made in the National Commission Minimum Programme. Otherwise, our 60 year old experiment with democracy can not be called an unqualified success

References

1. *Hindustan Times*, 28.02.08.
3. *Hindustan Times*, 11.08. 07.
2. *India Today*, Sep. 24, 2007, p. 43.
4. *Hindustan Times*, 28.02.08.
5. *India Today*, Sept. 24, 2007, p. 42.
6. *Ibid.*, p. 43.
8. *Ibid.*, pp. 44-45.
7. *Yojana*, May 2007, p. 49.
9. *Hindustan Times*, 02.08.08.
10. *Hindustan Times*, 09.03.2008.
11. *Hindustan Times*, 06.03.2008.
12. *Hindustan Times*, 25.02.2008.
13. *Hindustan Times*, 06.03.2008.

Index